Ultimate Git and GitHub for Modern Software Development

Unlock the Power of Git and GitHub Version Control and Collaborative Coding to Seamlessly Manage and Streamline Software Projects

Pravin Mishra

www.orangeava.com

First published: June 2024

Published by: Orange Education Pvt Ltd, AVA™

Address: 9, Daryaganj, Delhi, 110002, India

275 New North Road Islington Suite 1314 London,

N1 7AA, United Kingdom

ISBN: 978-81-97223-83-9

www.orangeava.com

Dedicated To

My Beloved Bade Papa, Badi Maa, and Sisters:

Bharat Mishra

Girja Devi

Rita Rai

Nita Mishra

My Strength and Support System

and

To my startup, The CloudAdvisory, a dream that took shape, inspiring me every day and fueling my desire to share knowledge and make a difference in the world of cloud IT. Your inception has been the drive behind this effort

About the Author

Pravin Mishra is an accomplished author, AWS Trainer, Mentor, and Cloud Computing Expert with over 14 years of experience in the IT industry. As the author of *Cloud Computing with* AWS and *Mastering* AWS *DevOps*, his books have garnered significant traction among students and professionals seeking to enhance their cloud skills. Pravin is an AWS Community Builder, recognized for his deep understanding of the AWS ecosystem and its applications.

Pravin currently serves as an Enterprise Architect at The CloudAdvisory, where he specializes in assisting customers with cloud migration and application modernization. He has a proven track record of success, having previously worked for renowned companies like Nordcloud, Ericsson, and Verizon, focusing on cloud migration to AWS and upskilling IT professionals.

With a passion for sharing knowledge, Pravin maintains an active YouTube channel (https://www.youtube.com/@awswithpravinmishra) and offers an Udemy course on different subjects (https://www.udemy.com/user/pravin-mishra-30/). His clear and practical writing style makes complex cloud computing concepts accessible to readers of all levels.

In the realm of Git and GitHub, Pravin has successfully implemented version control and collaborative coding practices in numerous projects, driving efficiency and productivity. His expertise in this area has been a valuable asset in his career as an IT professional and author. Beyond his professional achievements, Pravin is an avid organizer of meetup groups, fostering a vibrant community of developers and cloud enthusiasts. He actively participates in organizing events and facilitating knowledge sharing within these communities.

When he's not busy with work and writing, he enjoys quality time with his family, indulging in cooking, and engaging in outdoor activities such as badminton, running, and cycling.

About the Technical Reviewer

Thinknyx® Technologies is a team of professionals with years of experience in Information Technology. Their expertise ranges from software development to the management of IT infrastructure, cloud, automation, container management, web and app development, security, and professional services. Recognized as a reputable brand, Think Nyx® Technologies provides IT consulting services, offering comprehensive information technology and soft skills' training. Additionally, they offer talent acquisition and recruitment solutions to diverse organizations worldwide.

Mr. Kulbhushan Mayer, the Co-Founder of Thinknyx® Technologies, is a certified expert in DevOps, SRE, Cloud, and Containerisation, with over 17 years of IT experience. He has expertise in technologies such as Public/Private Cloud, Containers, Automation tools, Continuous Integration/Deployment/Delivery tools, Monitoring and Logging tools, and more. Mr. Mayer is passionate about sharing his technical expertise with a global audience through various forums, conferences, webinars, blogs, and LinkedIn. Furthermore, he has reviewed multiple books on Automation, DevOps, DevTools, and more for different vendors.

Acknowledgements

Writing this book has been an incredible journey, and its completion would not have been possible without the support and encouragement of many individuals.

First and foremost, I would like to express my deepest gratitude to my family – my wife Neha Mishra and son Priyansh Mishra – for their unwavering love, patience, and understanding throughout this endeavor. Their belief in me and their constant support have been my driving force.

I am immensely thankful to my colleagues and mentors, whose invaluable insights, knowledge, and experiences have enriched this book tremendously. Their guidance and constructive feedback have helped me refine and improve the content, ensuring that it remains practical and relevant.

I would also like to extend my heartfelt appreciation to the entire team at **Orange AVA** for their professionalism, dedication, and commitment to making this book a reality. Their expertise and attention to detail have been instrumental in shaping this work into a comprehensive and polished resource.

Last but not least, I am grateful to the countless developers, authors, and contributors who have shared their knowledge and experiences within the vibrant Git and GitHub communities. Their passion for collaboration and knowledge-sharing has inspired me and countless others on our respective journeys.

Finally, to the readers, thank you for choosing this book as your source of knowledge. May it be a valuable companion on your journey to mastering Git and navigating the dynamic world of Source Code Management System.

Preface

Git and GitHub have revolutionized the way software developers collaborate, manage code, and track changes. As technology continues to evolve, the need for efficient version control systems and collaborative platforms has become paramount. This book is designed to provide you with a comprehensive understanding of Git and GitHub, equipping you with the knowledge and skills necessary to navigate the ever-changing landscape of software development.

Whether you're a beginner embarking on your coding journey or an experienced developer seeking to enhance your existing skills, this book will serve as your guide. From the fundamental concepts of Git repositories and basic commands to advanced techniques and best practices, we will explore the intricacies of these powerful tools.

Chapter 1. Introduction: In this chapter, we will explore the basics of Git and GitHub, understanding their importance in the software development world. We will also cover the key terminologies and concepts that form the foundation for the rest of the book.

Chapter 2. Setting Up Git: This chapter will guide you through the process of installing and configuring Git on various operating systems. We will also discuss how to troubleshoot common installation issues and introduce Git GUI tools.

Chapter 3. Understanding Git Repositories: In this chapter, we will delve into the concept of Git repositories, both local and remote. You will learn how to create your first repository and work with files within it, laying the groundwork for version control.

Chapter 4. Basic Git Commands: In this chapter, we will cover the essential Git commands that are crucial for managing your codebase effectively. From checking the status of your repository to committing and viewing your Git history, you will gain a comprehensive understanding of the fundamental commands.

Chapter 5. Branching and Merging: This chapter will explore the powerful branching and merging capabilities of Git. You will learn how to create new branches, switch between them, and merge changes from one branch to another. We will also discuss how to resolve merge conflicts and best practices for branching and merging.

Chapter 6. Introduction to GitHub: In this chapter, you will be introduced to GitHub, the world's leading platform for hosting and collaborating on Git repositories. We will cover the importance of GitHub, key terminologies, and how to set up your GitHub account.

Chapter 7. Working Seamlessly with Both Git and GitHub: Here, we will learn how to integrate Git with GitHub, covering topics such as pushing and pulling changes, collaborating with others, and practical exercises to solidify your understanding.

Chapter 8. Advanced Git Techniques: This chapter will delve into advanced Git techniques, including rebasing, cherry-picking, bisecting, and stashing. You will learn how to leverage these powerful features to streamline your workflow and overcome complex challenges.

Chapter 9. GitOps: The Future of Operations: In this chapter, we will explore the concept of GitOps, a modern approach to managing infrastructure and deployments using Git principles. You will gain insights into the advantages of GitOps, tools and platforms supporting it, and real-world case studies.

Chapter 10. Best Practices with Git and GitHub: The final chapter will focus on best practices for using Git and GitHub effectively. You will learn techniques for crafting meaningful commit messages, keeping sensitive data out of repositories, pull request etiquettes, and conducting effective code reviews.

Ultimately, this book aims to equip you with the knowledge and skills necessary to become a proficient Git and GitHub user, enabling you to work efficiently, collaborate effectively, and contribute to the broader software development community.

Get a Free eBook

We hope you are enjoying your recently purchased book! Your feedback is incredibly valuable to us, and to all other readers looking for great books.

If you found this book helpful or enjoyable, we would truly appreciate it, if you could take a moment to leave a short review with a 5 star rating on Amazon. It helps us grow, and lets other readers discover our books.

As a thank you, we would love to send you a free digital copy of this book, and a **30%** discount code on your next cart value on our official websites:

www.orangeava.com

www.orangeava.in (For Indian Subcontinent)

☑ **Here's how:**

Leave a review for the book on Amazon.

Take a screenshot of your review, and send an email to **info@orangeava.com** (it can be just the confirmation screen).

Once, we receive your screenshot, we will send you the digital file, within 24 hours.

Thank you so much for your support – it means a lot to us!

Downloading the code bundles and colored images

Please follow the links or scan the QR codes to download the ***Code Bundles and Images*** of the book:

https://github.com/ava-orange-education/Ultimate-Git-and-GitHub-for-Modern-Software-Development

The code bundles and images of the book are also hosted on ***rebrand.ly/6h3sn6k***

In case there's an update to the code, it will be updated on the existing GitHub repository.

Errata

We take immense pride in our work at **Orange Education Pvt Ltd,** and follow best practices to ensure the accuracy of our content to provide an indulging reading experience to our subscribers. Our readers are our mirrors, and we use their inputs to reflect and improve upon human errors, if any, that may have occurred during the publishing processes involved. To let us maintain the quality and help us reach out to any readers who might be having difficulties due to any unforeseen errors, please write to us at :

errata@orangeava.com

Your support, suggestions, and feedback are highly appreciated.

DID YOU KNOW

Did you know that Orange Education Pvt Ltd offers eBook versions of every book published, with PDF and ePub files available? You can upgrade to the eBook version at **www.orangeava.com** and as a print book customer, you are entitled to a discount on the eBook copy. Get in touch with us at: **info@orangeava.com** for more details.

At **www.orangeava.com**, you can also read a collection of free technical articles, sign up for a range of free newsletters, and receive exclusive discounts and offers on AVA™ Books and eBooks.

PIRACY

If you come across any illegal copies of our works in any form on the internet, we would be grateful if you would provide us with the location address or website name. Please contact us at **info@orangeava.com** with a link to the material.

ARE YOU INTERESTED IN AUTHORING WITH US?

If there is a topic that you have expertise in, and you are interested in either writing or contributing to a book, please write to us at **business@orangeava.com**. We are on a journey to help developers and tech professionals to gain insights on the present technological advancements and innovations happening across the globe and build a community that believes Knowledge is best acquired by sharing and learning with others. Please reach out to us to learn what our audience demands and how you can be part of this educational reform. We also welcome ideas from tech experts and help them build learning and development content for their domains.

REVIEWS

Please leave a review. Once you have read and used this book, why not leave a review on the site that you purchased it from? Potential readers can then see and use your unbiased opinion to make purchase decisions. We at Orange Education would love to know what you think about our products, and our authors can learn from your feedback. Thank you!

For more information about Orange Education, please visit **www.orangeava.com**.

Table of Contents

CHAPTER 1
Introduction

Introduction

Welcome to this comprehensive tutorial on Git and GitHub! Let us explore the fundamentals.

Git is a version control system that tracks changes in the codebase, allowing multiple developers to collaborate seamlessly. It is like a time machine for your code, enabling you to revisit and undo any changes effortlessly. GitHub, on the other hand, is a web-based platform that hosts Git repositories. It adds a social layer to version control, facilitating collaboration among developers globally. Think of it as a virtual space where your code lives and thrives.

In the chapters that follow, we will explore Git commands, branching strategies, and how to resolve conflicts – all in straightforward terms. The goal is to demystify these concepts, making them accessible to everyone, regardless of their experience level. So, whether you are just beginning your coding journey, or a seasoned developer looking to enhance your version control skills, this guide is tailored for you. Together, let us navigate the world of Git and GitHub.

Structure

In this chapter, we will cover the following topics:

- Introduction to Git: The What and Why of Version Control
- Importance of Version Control
- Understanding Branching
- Understanding Merging
- Importance of Collaboration

Introduction to Git: The What and Why of Version Control

A common challenge faced by many developers is the handling of numerous changes and updates in coding projects. These changes could range from adding a new feature to fixing a small bug. As the projects grow, the need to keep track of these changes becomes even more important, and that is where Git comes in.

During the early days in the industry, it was challenging to manage every small change in the code being saved as a different version. Imagine having files named `project_v1`, `project_v2`, `project_final`, and `project_final_revised`. Not only was this confusing but it was also not scalable. Sharing these versions with teammates was another big hassle. If two people were working on the same project, it would often lead to overwritten work or lost code, leading to frustration and decreased productivity.

When I first came across Git, I realized it was not just another tool, but a solution to a problem that every developer faced. Git is a version control system designed to track changes in computer files, but is typically used by developers to track changes in their source code. With Git, I could make changes to my code and commit those changes. Each commit was like a snapshot of my code at the time. If I ever needed to go back to a previous version, Git made it easy. It was also not just about keeping track, but about collaboration. With Git, multiple developers could work on the same project without any overlap. Everyone could work in their own environment, make their own changes, and then merge those changes together in a coordinated manner.

For a beginner, Git may seem overwhelming at first. However, once you get the hang of it, it becomes second nature. The benefits of learning Git far outweigh the initial learning curve. For me, Git became more than just a tool – it became an integral part of my workflow. It enabled me to experiment without fear. If a new piece of code did not work out, I could easily revert to a previous version. It gave me freedom, flexibility, and most importantly, peace of mind.

With over 14 years in IT, I have seen trends come and go, but Git remains a constant. Its importance cannot be stressed enough, especially in today's context of fast-paced development cycles. Whether you are a solo developer working on a passion project, or a part of a large team in a multinational company, understanding Git thoroughly is crucial for anyone in the software development world.

Over the years, Git has carried me through many challenges. From accidental deletions to collaborating with teams across different time zones, Git has been my constant companion. Through the chapters that follow, I aim to share with you my knowledge, tips, and experiences of using Git, and hope to make your coding journey smoother and more efficient.

Understanding the Importance of Versions

To truly understand the importance of versions, let us think of them as different editions of a book. When a book is first published, that is its first version. As time goes on, the author might make changes based on feedback or new ideas, creating a new version. It remains the same core book, but contains some tweaks reflecting the author's revised intentions.

Now, let me share a bit about my IT journey from around 14 years ago. Back then, handling versions of applications was not as smooth as it is with Git today. Releasing an updated version was a complex process, involving manual tracking of changes to avoid mistakes. It was a tedious task to sift through lines of code just to identify what had changed from the last version.

Think about your favourite software applications. Developers constantly gather user feedback, fix bugs, and add new features, releasing a new version each time. Every version of an app reflects its growth and evolution. For instance, early versions of apps such as WhatsApp were mainly meant for messaging, but over time, additional features such as voice calls and video calls were introduced through new versions.

The idea of versioning extends to music as well. A song might have studio, live, or acoustic versions, each offering a unique experience, while being rooted in the original composition.

In IT and software development, versioning is crucial. Every software or application undergoes changes, from fixing typos to overhauling interfaces. Without a system like Git, managing these changes would be chaotic. Git is more than a tool, it is a structured way to track changes, allowing developers to work together without conflicts. Each change is documented, making it easy to review, merge, or revert, if needed.

In essence, versions show the evolution of a product, whether it is a book, an application, or a song. They document their journey, growth, and refinement over time. In our digital age, in which software is constantly evolving, a robust system like Git is not only beneficial, but essential. Git ensures that managing versions is seamless, efficient, and reliable. Understanding this is the first step to mastering version control with Git.

Importance of Version Control

The IT industry thrives on collaboration. Over 14 years, countless projects, big and small, have succeeded through teamwork. Collaboration brings together diverse minds and skills to achieve a shared goal, but with collaboration comes complexity.

Let us understand this with an example:

Imagine you are back in school. It is the final year, and you are working on an important school project. This project is crucial for your grades, and multiple classmates are involved. Each one of you has a specific task, such as writing content, drawing diagrams, providing references, and more. As the days pass, everyone starts to contribute. Papers start piling up, diagrams get drawn and redrawn, and before you know it, there is a stack of notes, drafts, and final versions. In this pile, James' final version of a diagram might be mistakenly replaced by Sophia's initial draft. Alice's well-researched content might be overwritten by Bob's first thoughts. The chaos is undeniable.

Now, imagine this at a much larger scale in software development. Multiple developers, sometimes in the hundreds, working on thousands of lines of code, making multiple changes every single day. The sheer volume of changes and the pace at which they are made is enough to overwhelm anyone. Accidentally overwriting someone's code, losing track of which version is the latest, or simply trying to figure out who made a particular change can become a nightmare. There is a greater need for a system that provides clarity, organization, and control.

That is where version control comes in!

Version control, as its name implies, helps control and manage different versions of your work. It is like having a detailed diary of your project that notes down every single change, including who made it, and when. If mistakes are made, it allows you to turn back and restore a previous state. If you wish to understand who contributed what to the current version, the diary provides clear answers. In essence, it is the safety net and record-keeper for your project.

Now, speaking from personal experience, while there are several tools out there that offer version control, Git stands out in its efficiency, simplicity, and widespread adoption.

Understanding Git

Git is a version control system, also known as Source Code Management system.

Let us first talk about version control. It is a system used to manage different versions of a file, set of files, code, book, and so on. Controlling versions becomes even more important when multiple people work on a single product. It allows multiple people to collaborate on the same files without accidentally overwriting each other's work, and it also provides a history of changes made to the files over time.

In version control, every time a change is made to a file, the system saves a new version of the file. This means that if a mistake is made or something needs to be changed, it is always possible to go back to an earlier version of the file.

As mentioned in the beginning of this chapter, Git is a version control system. With Git, a developer can keep track of the changes made to their code, and multiple developers can work on the same code without disturbing or overwriting each other's code.

Let us understand this with the help of one example.

Suppose you are a software developer in an organization, and you are working on an application. A team of developers is writing code, and, being a part of the team, you are also writing and editing the code. One way to manage the code is that everyone in the team has access to the original code and they can make the changes they want. Later, everyone submits their changes, and all the new changes will be added to the original code. This is not an easy task. While it may be possible in situations that involve two or three developers, it becomes much more complicated if there are, say, 10 or 15 developers working on the same project. This is therefore not the most efficient or safe way, as you might lose the original code. That is when you may like to use a version control system to manage the code. Version control ensures that every new change made in the code is saved as a new version and you can always go back to the previous versions if you are not happy with the new changes. Basically, we can create multiple versions of the code, and switch to any version any time.

Need for Git

The most important thing that Git provides is version control, that is, the ability to track and manage changes to the source code.

Let us imagine that you are working on a document on your computer, and you want to make some changes to it. You make some edits, save the document, and then realise you made a mistake. In this case, you might have to think around and manually remove the changes you made or start over from scratch. Right?

Is there any way to go one step or a couple of steps back?

Yes, you can use the **Undo** feature in your text editor to go back one step or multiple. Right?

So, you go back to the previous versions of your document.

Git is similarly a widely used version control system in software development that helps you to go back to any previous version of your code.

It also allows you to work on the code without changing the original code, This is called branching.

Understanding Branching

Branching is the practice of creating a separate copy of source code that diverges from the main source code. Each copy, called a branch, works independently.

Let us understand this with an example:

Let us say you have created a website with your friend. One day, you come up with an idea for a new feature that you want to add to the website. However, you do not want to make changes directly to the main code as the website might stop working. Thus, you want to avoid making changes directly to the main code.

In such a case, you can create a branch, and make any changes you want on a branch code, such as adding a new page to the website or changing the layout. You can test the changes and see how they look without affecting the main code Once you are happy with the changes, you can merge the branch back into the main code, and the new feature will be added to the website. Your friend can then see the changes and give feedback or make additional changes, if needed.

Using branches in this way allows you to experiment with new features or changes without affecting the main code.

Now, as you have new code on a branch, this code needs to be updated to the main code as well. This is called **merging**.

Understanding Merging

Merging is the process of combining changes made to two different branches of code into a single branch. It is like taking two different versions of a document and combining them into a new version.

Let us understand this by using the previous example:

You have created your own branch to work on different features of the code. Once you have made the changes and are happy with your code, you can initiate the processes of merging to combine your branches back into the main code.

This means that all the changes made in your branch will be combined into a single version of the code.

Merging is important because it allows different team members to work on different parts of the code at the same time, without interfering with each other's work. It also allows you to experiment with different changes and features without affecting the main code until you are ready to merge.

However, there is a catch there. It is important to be careful while merging, because if there are conflicts between the changes made in different branches, it can cause problems in the code. It is therefore important to make sure that you test the merged code thoroughly before deploying it to make sure everything is working properly.

As you may have noticed, these features offer the capacity to collaboratively work as a team.

Importance of Collaboration

Collaboration is the practice of working with other developers, stakeholders, and team members to build and maintain the software application project.

As you have seen in the previous examples, it makes it easy to work in a team without worries about code conflict.

Each person in a team can work on different parts of the code at the same time without interfering with each other's work. You can create branches to experiment with new features or changes, and merge them back into the main code when you are ready.

This makes it easier to work together as a team and ensure that everyone is on the same page. You can see the changes that your teammates have made and give feedback or make additional changes if needed.

Conclusion

In this chapter, we have learned that Git helps keep track of changes in our code. It makes working together with other developers smooth, and not confusing.

GitHub is like a home for our code on the internet, where everyone can join in and work together. In the following chapters, we will dive into more details about Git commands, and how to handle some common problems that may come up in its use. Do not worry if it seems a bit tricky at first – it is like learning to ride a bike. Once you get the hang of it, it becomes second nature.

This wraps up the content for this chapter. Moving forward, our focus will shift to the installation and configuration of Git. Stay tuned for a hands-on exploration of setting up and optimizing Git for your needs!

CHAPTER 2
Setting Up Git

Introduction

Welcome! If you've reached this chapter, you are likely eager to set up Git on your machine and dive into the world of version control. This chapter will guide you through every step of that journey.

Let's proceed with installing Git on your machine.

Structure

In this chapter, we will cover the following topics:

- Installing Git Step-by-Step (Demo)
- Configuring Git for First-Time Use
- Troubleshooting Common Installation Issues
- Git GUI Tools
- Setting Up SSH with Git
- Verifying Your Installation
- Explaining Git Configurations
- Tips and Best Practices

Installing Git Step-by-Step (Demo)

Git can be installed on a variety of operating systems, including Windows, MacOS, and Linux. Please adhere to the steps applicable to your OS and disregard those that are irrelevant.

Installing Git on Windows

Here are the steps for installing Git on Windows:

Downloading the Installer

To begin, visit the official Git website at https://git-scm.com/download/win to download the installer (see *Figure* 2.1) suited for Windows:

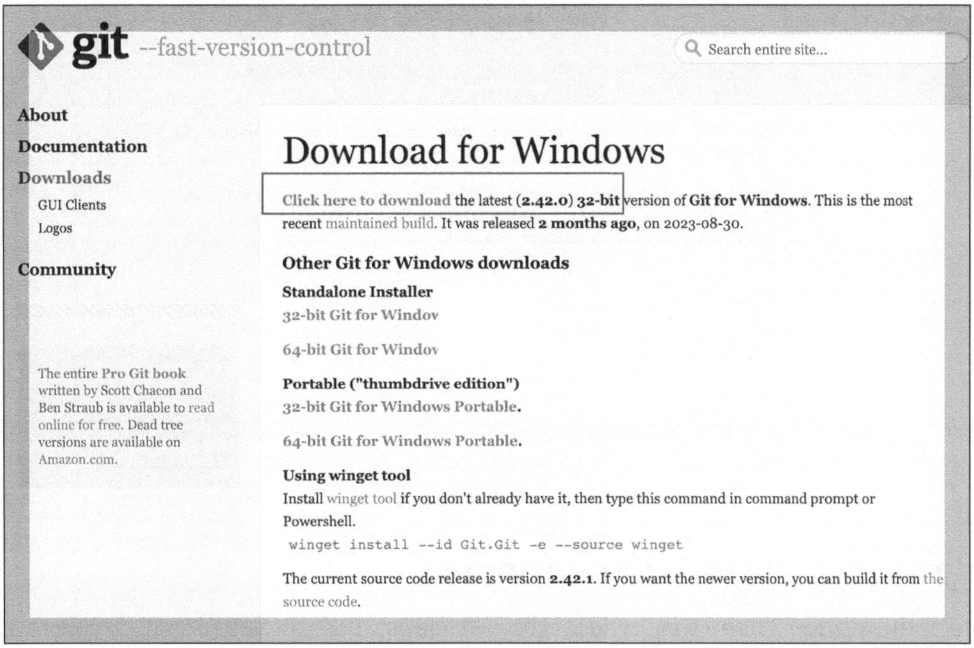

***Figure* 2.1**: *Downloading the Installer*

Running the Installer

After the download is complete, launch the installer. This will prompt a series of setup windows to appear.

Customizing Installation Settings

While the default settings are suitable for most users, it is advisable to pay close attention to the following:

Choosing the text editor for Git

The default text editor for Git is Vim. However, if you are not familiar with it, you might opt for a more intuitive editor such as Notepad++ or Visual Studio Code (see *Figure* 2.2):

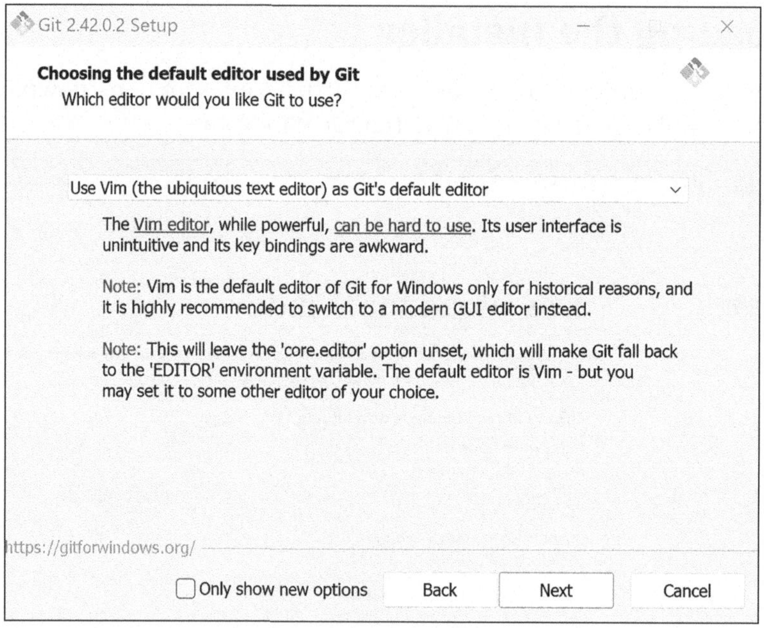

Figure 2.2: *Choosing the editor*

Adjusting your PATH environment

Select the option "**`Use Git from the Windows Command Prompt`**" for seamless integration (see *Figure 2.3*):

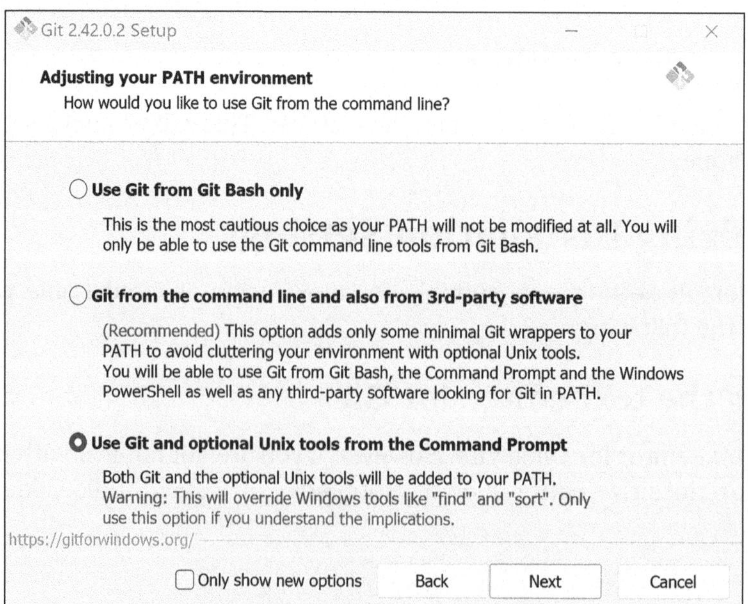

Figure 2.3: *Command Prompt option*

Finalizing installation

Follow the remaining prompts, to complete the installation process. Congratulations! Git is now installed on your Windows machine (see *Figure* 2.4):

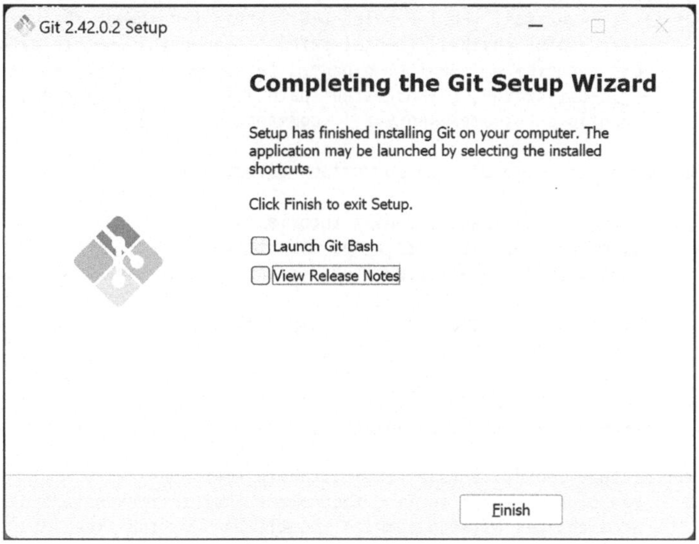

Figure 2.4: *Git is installed*

Installing Git on macOS

macOS is popular primarily because of its UNIX-based architecture.

To set up Git, follow these steps:

Using Homebrew

If Homebrew is already installed simply type `brew install git` in your terminal as shown here (see *Figure* 2.5):

```
pravinmishra@pravin-MacBook-Pro ~ brew install git
==> Downloading https://formulae.brew.sh/api/formula.jws.json
curl: (28) Operation too slow. Less than 100 bytes/sec transferred the last 5 seconds

Warning: formula.jws.json: update failed, falling back to cached version.
==> Downloading https://formulae.brew.sh/api/cask.jws.json
curl: (28) Operation too slow. Less than 100 bytes/sec transferred the last 5 seconds

Warning: cask.jws.json: update failed, falling back to cached version.
Warning: git 2.42.1 is already installed and up-to-date.
To reinstall 2.42.1, run:
  brew reinstall git
pravinmishra@pravin-MacBook-Pro ~
```

Figure 2.5: *'brew install git' command*

After the preceding commands have run successfully type "**`git --help`**" in a Terminal. This command should display a list all Git commands as shown in *Figure 2.6*, indicating successful installation:

```
pravinmishra@pravin-MacBook-Pro ~ git --help
usage: git [-v | --version] [-h | --help] [-C <path>] [-c <name>=<value>]
           [--exec-path[=<path>]] [--html-path] [--man-path] [--info-path]
           [-p | --paginate | -P | --no-pager] [--no-replace-objects] [--bare]
           [--git-dir=<path>] [--work-tree=<path>] [--namespace=<name>]
           [--config-env=<name>=<envvar>] <command> [<args>]

These are common Git commands used in various situations:

start a working area (see also: git help tutorial)
   clone     Clone a repository into a new directory
   init      Create an empty Git repository or reinitialize an existing one

work on the current change (see also: git help everyday)
   add       Add file contents to the index
   mv        Move or rename a file, a directory, or a symlink
   restore   Restore working tree files
   rm        Remove files from the working tree and from the index

examine the history and state (see also: git help revisions)
   bisect    Use binary search to find the commit that introduced a bug
   diff      Show changes between commits, commit and working tree, etc
   grep      Print lines matching a pattern
   log       Show commit logs
   show      Show various types of objects
   status    Show the working tree status

grow, mark and tweak your common history
   branch    List, create, or delete branches
   commit    Record changes to the repository
   merge     Join two or more development histories together
   rebase    Reapply commits on top of another base tip
   reset     Reset current HEAD to the specified state
   switch    Switch branches
   tag       Create, list, delete or verify a tag object signed with GPG

collaborate (see also: git help workflows)
   fetch     Download objects and refs from another repository
   pull      Fetch from and integrate with another repository or a local branch
   push      Update remote refs along with associated objects

'git help -a' and 'git help -g' list available subcommands and some
concept guides. See 'git help <command>' or 'git help <concept>'
to read about a specific subcommand or concept.
See 'git help git' for an overview of the system.
pravinmishra@pravin-MacBook-Pro ~
```

***Figure 2.6**: Git installed successfully*

Manual Installation: Visit official Git website at https://git-scm.com /download/mac to download the macOS installer. Launch the installer and follow the prompts.

(*Figure* 2.7) illustrates we have shown the various methods for installing Git on MacOS:

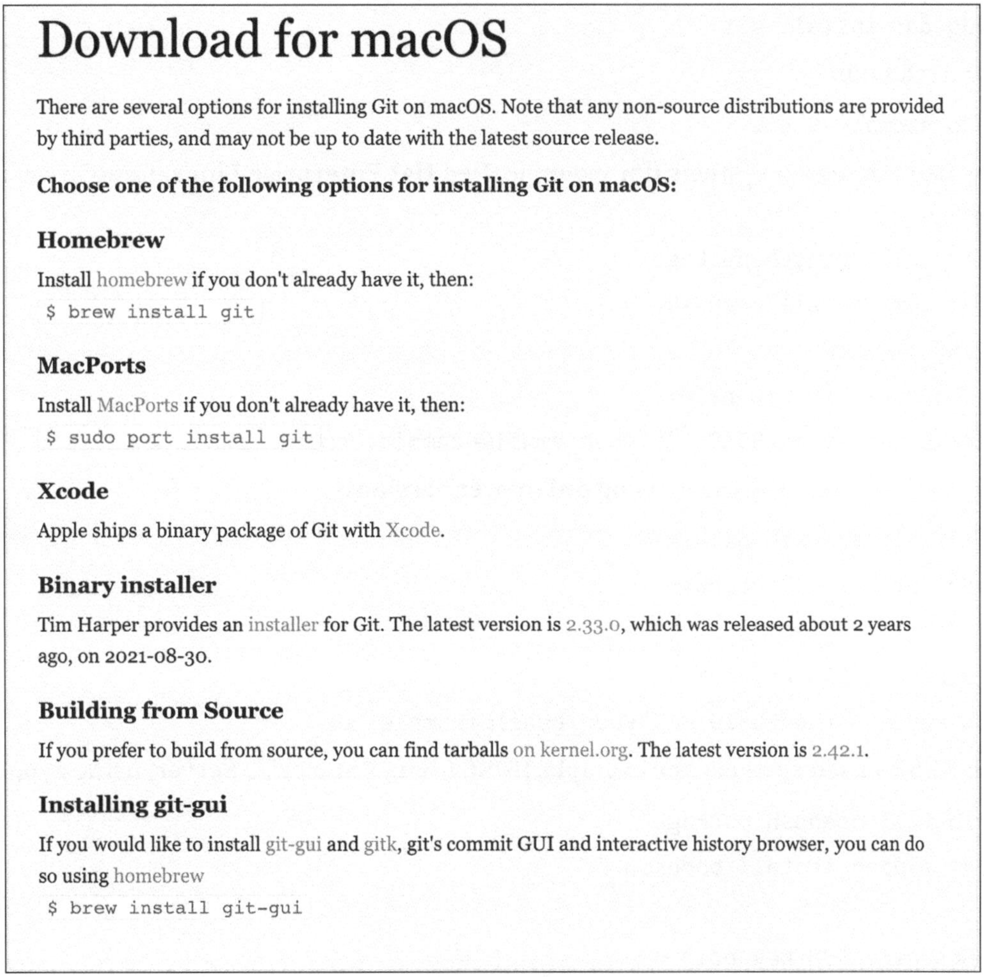

Download for macOS

There are several options for installing Git on macOS. Note that any non-source distributions are provided by third parties, and may not be up to date with the latest source release.

Choose one of the following options for installing Git on macOS:

Homebrew

Install homebrew if you don't already have it, then:

```
$ brew install git
```

MacPorts

Install MacPorts if you don't already have it, then:

```
$ sudo port install git
```

Xcode

Apple ships a binary package of Git with Xcode.

Binary installer

Tim Harper provides an installer for Git. The latest version is 2.33.0, which was released about 2 years ago, on 2021-08-30.

Building from Source

If you prefer to build from source, you can find tarballs on kernel.org. The latest version is 2.42.1.

Installing git-gui

If you would like to install git-gui and gitk, git's commit GUI and interactive history browser, you can do so using homebrew

```
$ brew install git-gui
```

Figure 2.7: *Installing Git on MacOS*

Installing Git on Linux

Setting up Git is straightforward. Here is how you can do using Package Managers:

Using Package Managers

For Debian/Ubuntu

```
sudo apt-get install git
```

For Fedora

```
sudo dnf install git
```

For Arch Linux

```
sudo pacman -S git
```

For Red Hat-based systems (for example, Red Hat Enterprise Linux, CentOS) using `yum`

```
# Install openssh package
sudo yum install openssh

# Generate SSH key pair
ssh-keygen -t ed25519 -C "your_email@example.com"
```

For Red Hat-based systems using dnf (newer versions)

```
# Install openssh package
sudo dnf install openssh

# Generate SSH key pair
ssh-keygen -t ed25519 -C "your_email@example.com"
```

For SUSE-based systems (for example, SUSE Linux Enterprise Server) using zypper

```
# Install openssh package
sudo zypper install openssh

# Generate SSH key pair
ssh-keygen -t ed25519 -C "your_email@example.com"
```

Compiling from Source

Alternatively, you can compile Git from the source. To do so, visit the official Git source page at https://git-scm.com/download/sources, download the source, extract it, and then follow the instructions provided in the README file.

Configuring Git for First-Time Use

Once Git is installed, it is essential to configure a few settings to ensure smooth operations.

Setting up User Information

Before making any commits, Git must identify the user, ensuring accountability for every change. To set up user information, use the following commands:

```
git config --global user.name "Your Name"

git config --global user.email "youremail@example.com"
```

Next, run the preceding commands in the Terminal to see the output (see *Figure* 2.8):

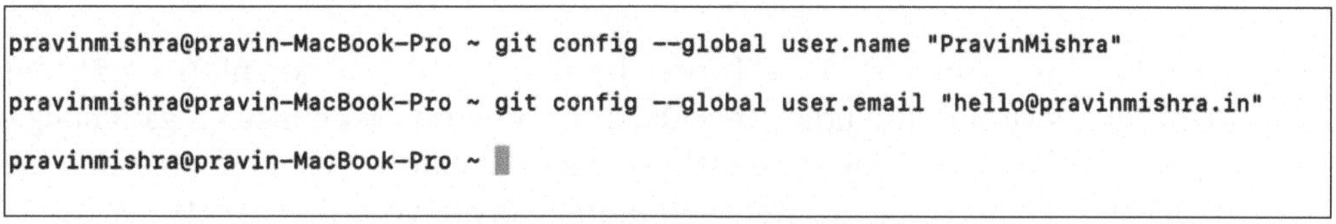

```
pravinmishra@pravin-MacBook-Pro ~ git config --global user.name "PravinMishra"
pravinmishra@pravin-MacBook-Pro ~ git config --global user.email "hello@pravinmishra.in"
pravinmishra@pravin-MacBook-Pro ~
```

***Figure* 2.8**: *Running commands*

Choosing a Default Editor

Whenever Git requires you to input a longer message, such as commit messages, it will use an editor. By default, this might be *Vim*. If you have another preference, such as *Nano*, you can set it up with as follows:

Configuring the Nano Editor

```
git config --global core.editor nano
```

Next, run the preceding command in the Terminal see the output (see *Figure* 2.9):

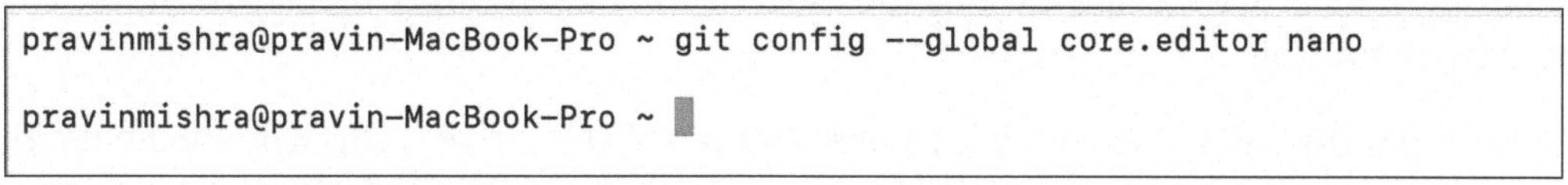

```
pravinmishra@pravin-MacBook-Pro ~ git config --global core.editor nano
pravinmishra@pravin-MacBook-Pro ~
```

***Figure* 2.9**: *Run command 'git config --global core.editor nano'*

Configuring Visual Studio Code Editor

Ensure that Visual Studio Code (VS code) is already installed on your system. To configure VS Code, you need to install the "`Code`" command. Follow these steps:

1. Install `code` from VSCode commander (*Shift* + *Command* + P).

2. Search for `code` using the following command.

Shell Command: `Install code command in 'PATH'`

3. Install it.

Afterword, run the following commands in the Terminal to configure Git with the new editor:

```
$ git config --global core.editor "code --wait"
$ git config --global -e
```

That's all.

When executing this command, Git will open the global configuration file (`~/.gitconfig` on most Unix-like systems, including macOS, or `C:\Users\<username>\.gitconfig` on Windows) in Visual Studio Code (or another specified editor). This file contains your global Git settings allowing you to view and modify any of your global settings such as user information (name and email), default branch naming, aliases, and more.

Now, you have successfully configured Visual Studio Code Editor with Git.

Handling Line Endings

When working in a team, individuals use different types of computers, such as Windows, Mac, or Linux, and work together. Each operating system has its own way of indicating the end of a line in a text file: Windows uses a combination of two characters (`CRLF - \r\n`), while both macOS and Linux use a single character (`LF - \n`).

As these operating systems do not agree on how to mark the end of lines, files can appear messy or may not function correctly when accessed by others. Therefore, ensuring that everyone uses the same system for line endings helps everyone work together smoothly.

To address this, you can set with `core.autocrlf`. Once set, Git will automatically convert LF to CRLF when you check out code on your local machine if you are on Windows. This is because Windows expects CRLF as the line ending in text files.

Now to configure this for your respective operating system, use the following commands.:

On Windows

```
git config --global core.autocrlf true
```

On macOS and Linux

```
git config --global core.autocrlf input
```

Run the preceding command in the Terminal to see the output (see *Figure* 2.10):

```
pravinmishra@pravin-MacBook-Pro ~ git config --global core.autocrlf input

pravinmishra@pravin-MacBook-Pro ~ X
```

***Figure* 2.10**: *Running the command 'git config --global core.autocrlf input'*

Setting up and configuring Git has presented some challenges, especially when working with proxy servers or in workplaces where the network is tightly controlled. Newcomers often find it difficult to use Vim, which is the default editor for Git, and sometimes struggle to exit it. It's a good practice to choose your favorite editor immediately after installing Git to avoid these kinds of issues.

Troubleshooting Common Installation Issues

While the installation of Git is mostly smooth, occasionally, there are occasional bumps on the road. Here are some common issues and their solutions:

"Git is not recognized as an internal or external command"

This error on Windows usually means Git isn't added to your PATH. To resolve this issue, revisit the installation steps and ensure that you choose the option to add Git to your PATH.

Issues with SSH Keys on GitHub

Once you move to GitHub, managing SSH keys can be a challenge. If you face authentication issues, double-check your SSH keys. Ensure that the key on your machine matches the one you've provided to GitHub.

Git GUI Tools

Although using the command line to work with Git is preferred by some, it is evident that visual interfaces can significantly help beginners or anyone who prefers a graphical representation of their work. Over time, numerous tools with graphical interfaces have been developed to make working with Git easier and more straightforward.

Now let's look at some of these tools.

GitKraken

GitKraken is a tool that works across different computer systems and has a colorful interface. This makes tasks such as creating branches and merging changes easy to understand visually. It is available at https://www.gitkraken.com/.

After opening the provided link, you will directed to the following page (see *Figure* 2.11.):

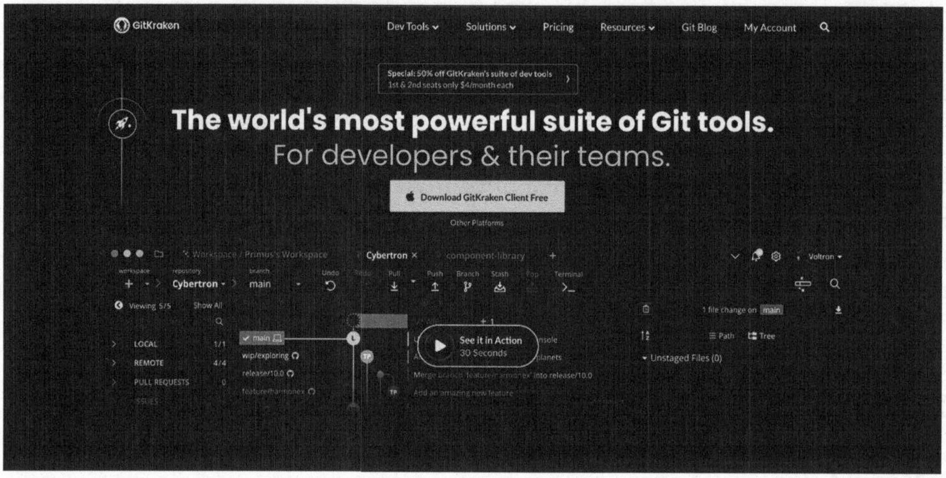

Figure 2.11: GitKraken

Sourcetree

Sourcetree is developed by Atlassian, the same company behind Bitbucket. Sourcetree simplifies Git operations without requiring users to remember command-line syntax. It is available at https://www.sourcetreeapp.com/.

After opening the provided link, you will be directed to the following page (see *Figure* 2.12.):

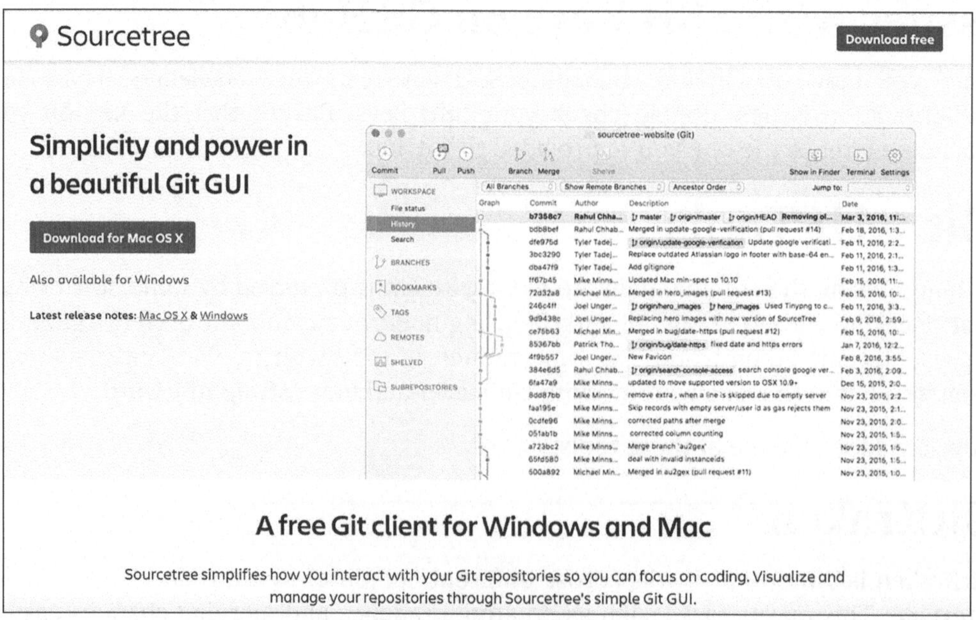

Figure 2.12: Sourcetree

GitHub Desktop

If you are using GitHub, this tool provides a seamless integration with your repositories, simplifying commits, pulls, and other operations. It is available at https://desktop.github.com/.

After opening the provided link, you will directed to the following page (see *Figure* 2.13.):

***Figure* 2.13**: *GitHub Desktop*

Setting Up SSH with Git

It is crucial to understand the importance of keeping communications safe, especially when working with and sharing code. This has led to the value of using strong security measures, such as setting up SSH (Secure Shell) with Git. SSH helps create a secure connection between your computer and the code stored online. It protects your work from unauthorized access. Furthermore, it simplifies the process of updating or accessing the latest version of your code, proving to be a must-have tool for developers who want to keep their work secure and private.

Now, let's explore the steps required to set up SSH with Git.

Generating SSH Keys

Here are the steps to generate SSH keys:

Open your terminal or command prompt, and run the following command:

```
ssh-keygen -t ed25519 -C "your_email@example.com".
```

The `ssh-keygen` command is used to generate SSH key pairs for authentication.

Let's break down the specific arguments used in the following command:

```
ssh-keygen -t ed25519 -C
```

- **`-t ed25519`**: This specifies the type of key to create. In this case, it is using the ed25519 algorithm, which is a modern and secure elliptic curve algorithm for generating SSH keys. Ed25519 keys are considered to be more secure and efficient compared to traditional RSA keys.
- **`-C "your_email@example.com"`**: This option allows you to add a comment or label to the key. While not mandatory, it is a good practice to include a comment to help you identify the key later, especially if multiple keys are present. In this example, the comment is set to the email address associated with the key.

In summary:

- `-t ed25519`: This specifies the type of key to generate (ed25519 algorithm).
- `-C "your_email@example.com"`: This adds a comment or label to the key for identification purposes.

When you run the preceding command, `ssh-keygen` will prompt you for the location to save the key pair (the default location is typically `~/.ssh/id_ed25519` for the private key and `~/.ssh/id_ed25519.pub` for the public key). If you do not want to overwrite an existing key pair, you can provide a different file name during the prompt.

This command generates a new SSH key pair using the Ed25519 algorithm, providing a secure and efficient authentication method. It also allows you to associate an optional comment for easy identification.

Finally, this creates a new SSH key using the provided email address.

Now, run this command in the Terminal to see the output (see *Figure 2.14*):

```
pravinmishra@pravin-MacBook-Pro ~  ssh-keygen -t ed25519 -C "hello@pravinmishra.in"
Generating public/private ed25519 key pair.
Enter file in which to save the key (/Users/sonali/.ssh/id_ed25519): Enter passphrase (empty for no passphrase):
Enter passphrase (empty for no passphrase):
Enter same passphrase again:
Your identification has been saved in Enter passphrase (empty for no passphrase):
Your public key has been saved in Enter passphrase (empty for no passphrase):.pub
The key fingerprint is:
SHA256:OyVRC5eWxqdxbeOsm70um3CW+Z9ntj5hkWvsY2rXn3g hello@pravinmishra.in
The key's randomart image is:
+--[ED25519 256]--+
|        ..oo .   |
|         +B.o +  |
|        .o.= + ..|
|         ..   oo |
|        S .  .. o|
|         +  .o * |
|        o . =++ o|
|         . +++oEB|
|            +*XXO|
+----[SHA256]-----+
pravinmishra@pravin-MacBook-Pro ~
```

Figure 2.14: *Running the command run ssh-keygen -t ed25519 -C "your_email@example.com"*

Adding Your SSH Key to the `ssh-agent`

Before adding SSH key to the **`ssh-agent`**, let us understand the benefits of using **`ssh-agent`**.

Benefits of using `ssh-agent`

`ssh-agent` is a program that manages Secure Shell (SSH) keys and their passphrases. It offers several benefits, making the authentication process more convenient and secure:

- **Single Sign-On Experience**: `ssh-agent` enables a single sign-on experience for SSH sessions. Once you add your private key to the agent, you do not need to re-enter your passphrase for each new SSH connection during the agent's session.
- **Passphrase Protection**: Although `ssh-agent` avoids repeated passphrase prompts during its session, it still keeps your private keys passphrase-protected. This means that your keys remain secure, and you only need to unlock them once per agent session.
- **Key Lifetime Management**: The agent can manage the lifecycle of your SSH keys. It can automatically expire keys after a specified period, adding an extra layer of security. This helps in minimizing the risk associated with long-lived, static keys.
- **Reduced Credential Exposure**: When using `ssh-agent`, private keys are stored in memory rather than on disk. This reduces the risk of unauthorized access to your private keys since they are not persistently stored in files.
- **Agent Forwarding**: `ssh-agent` supports agent forwarding, allowing you to use the same credentials to log in to multiple servers without storing your private key on each one. This is particularly useful when working with a chain of servers, such as when using a bastion host.
- **Integration with GUIs**: `ssh-agent` integrates well with **graphical user interfaces (GUIs)**. This is beneficial when using SSH from applications that have a graphical interface, as it allows a seamless and secure SSH authentication process.
- **Convenient for Scripts and Automation**: When scripting or automating SSH connections, `ssh-agent` can simplify the process. Scripts can use the agent to manage keys without the need to embed plaintext keys directly in the scripts, enhancing security.

While it is possible to use SSH without `ssh-agent` by entering passphrases repeatedly or by storing private keys without passphrase protection, using `ssh-agent` provides a balance between convenience and security. It allows users to manage and use their SSH keys more efficiently while maintaining a higher level of protection for those keys.

To start the SSH agent in the background, use `eval "$(ssh-agent -s)"` and then add your private key: `ssh-add ~/.ssh/id_ed25519` as shown in *Figure 2.15*:

```
[pravinmishra@pravin-MacBook-Pro ~ eval "$(ssh-agent -s)"
Agent pid 12849
[pravinmishra@pravin-MacBook-Pro ~ ssh-add ~/.ssh/id_ed255]19
```

***Figure 2.15**: Adding private key*

Now that everything is set up on your local computer, the next step is to add your SSH key to GitHub.

Adding the SSH Key to GitHub

To add your SSH key to GitHub, first go to your GitHub account. Click on your profile icon in the upper right corner and select **`Settings`** from the dropdown. In the **`Settings`** menu, navigate to the **`SSH keys`** section.

Here, you will have the option to add a new SSH key. Simply copy the content of your public key, which is usually found in the `~/.ssh/id_ed25519.pub` file, and paste it into the designated area to complete the process:

***Figure 2.16**: Adding a new SSH key*

Now, we have added the SSH key successfully (see *Figure 2.17*):

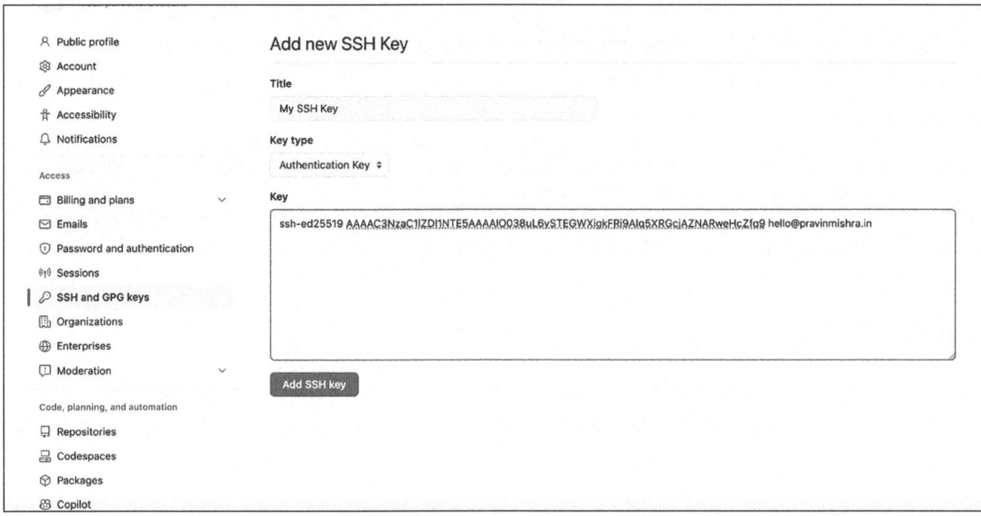

***Figure 2.17**: Added a new SSH key*

Great, let us proceed to verify your installation.

Verifying your Installation

It is always a good practice to ensure everything is in order after an installation. Here is a simple way to verify that Git is ready to go:

Open your Terminal or Git Bash (for Windows users) and type `git --version` (see *Figure 2.18*). This will display the version of Git you have installed, confirming that the installation was successful:

***Figure 2.18**: Running the command 'git --version'*

And there you have it! With Git installed and configured on your system, you are all set to dive deeper into the world of version control.

Explaining Git Configurations

Over the years, it has been found that mastering the configurations can significantly enhance your Git experience. These configurations are stored in the `.gitconfig` file, usually located in your home directory. The file holds global configurations:

Alias Setup

You can set up shortcuts for lengthy commands. For instance, using `git config --global alias.co` checkout allows you to use Git co as a shorthand for git checkout (see *Figure* 2.19):

```
pravinmishra@pravin-MacBook-Pro ~ git config --global alias.co
pravinmishra@pravin-MacBook-Pro ~
```

Figure 2.19: *Running the command 'git config --global alias.co checkout'*

Color UI

Make your Git experience colorful. By default, Git is colorless, but `git config --global colour.ui true` adds `colours to command outputs` (see *Figure* 2.19), making them more readable:

```
pravinmishra@pravin-MacBook-Pro ~ git config --global colour.ui true adds colours to command outputs
usage: git config [<options>]

Config file location
    --global              use global config file
    --system              use system config file
    --local               use repository config file
    --worktree            use per-worktree config file
    -f, --file <file>     use given config file
    --blob <blob-id>      read config from given blob object

Action
    --get                 get value: name [value-pattern]
    --get-all             get all values: key [value-pattern]
    --get-regexp          get values for regexp: name-regex [value-pattern]
    --get-urlmatch        get value specific for the URL: section[.var] URL
    --replace-all         replace all matching variables: name value [value-pattern]
    --add                 add a new variable: name value
    --unset               remove a variable: name [value-pattern]
    --unset-all           remove all matches: name [value-pattern]
    --rename-section      rename section: old-name new-name
    --remove-section      remove a section: name
    -l, --list            list all
    --fixed-value         use string equality when comparing values to 'value-pattern'
    -e, --edit            open an editor
    --get-color           find the color configured: slot [default]
    --get-colorbool       find the color setting: slot [stdout-is-tty]

Type
    -t, --type <type>     value is given this type
    --bool                value is "true" or "false"
    --int                 value is decimal number
    --bool-or-int         value is --bool or --int
    --bool-or-str         value is --bool or string
    --path                value is a path (file or directory name)
    --expiry-date         value is an expiry date

Other
    -z, --null            terminate values with NUL byte
    --name-only           show variable names only
    --includes            respect include directives on lookup
    --show-origin         show origin of config (file, standard input, blob, command line)
    --show-scope          show scope of config (worktree, local, global, system, command)
    --default <value>     with --get, use default value when missing entry

pravinmishra@pravin-MacBook-Pro ~
```

Figure 2.20: Colour UI

Tips and Best Practices

Some tips and best practices that can be followed for an enhanced user experience are as follows:

- **Regularly Update Git**: Software including Git, evolves over time. Regular updates ensure you benefit from the latest features and security patches.
- **Avoid Running as an Administrator**: Especially on Windows, running Git as an administrator can create files with elevated permissions. This can complicate file management and introduce potential security risks.
- **Commit Often**: This is crucial, as regular commits with clear messages help track changes and make troubleshooting easier.

Conclusion

Now that you have installed and configured Git, you are all set to embark on your journey into version control. Remember, Git is a powerful tool, and with great power comes great responsibility. Always ensure you are making meaningful commits and working collaboratively. In the next chapter, we will dive deeper into Git repositories and essential commands to elevate your Git knowledge.

CHAPTER 3
Understanding Git Repositories

Introduction

In the previous chapter, we set the stage by installing and configuring Git on our machines. Now, it's time to take the next step and dive into the world of Git - the repository. Throughout over 14 years, one thing has remained consistent: the power of understanding the basics. When it comes to Git, understanding repositories is as basic (and vital) as it gets.

Structure

In this chapter, we will cover the following topics:

- Git Repository and Its Importance
- Difference Between Local and Remote Repositories
- Creating Your Very First Repository
- Creating a File Inside a Git Repository

Understanding the Git Repository

A Git repository is a place where Git stores and tracks changes to your code. Think of it as a *database* for your code.

Imagine you are working on a project with a group of people. You might all be making changes to the code simultaneously, and you need a way to keep track of those changes. That's where Git comes in - it allows you to create a repository to store all the changes and versions of your code.

For example, let's say you are developing a website and decide to create a Git repository to store your code. Each time you make a change to the code, such as adding a new feature or fixing a bug, and you send those changes to the Git repository,

Git remembers all of these changes. You can even revert to previous versions of the code if needed.

So basically, a git repository is the collection of files, codes, documentation, and other assets related to a specific project. Think of it as a folder on your computer that contains all the project files and folders, except that Git tracks every change made to these files over time. It helps developers to save and manage all the source code in a single place. It can also track changes in the files available in the Git repository.

We can create a Git repository on our computer or local system; these repositories are known as local Git repositories. Alternatively, we can create remote Git repositories on a remote system, which can then be accessed over the network.

Let's talk more about local Git repositories.

A local Git repository is a place on your own computer or system where you can store and manage your code using Git. It is like a special folder that Git uses to keep track of changes you make to your code.

As discussed earlier, we could create a Git repository on our local system, which means, any of our working file directories can be converted into a Git repository. Directories are nothing but folders or spaces on your local system that you can use to store files.

Let's understand this with our previous example of a website.

As you are working on a website, and you want to use Git to keep track of your progress. You can create a local Git repository on your computer and add all the website codes and files to it. As you work on the project, Git will keep track of every change you make to the files, so you can easily go back and see what you did at any point in time.

The great thing about having a local Git repository is that you can work on your code even when you are not connected to the internet.

In case you want to put your code in a remote Git repository, you can make changes to your code, save them to the local repository, and then push them to a remote repository like the one hosted on GitHub when you have an internet connection. This way, people at different locations will be able to contribute to building your website.

Distributed Version Control System (DVCS) and Git

Version control systems are crucial for collaborative software development, enabling multiple contributors to work on a project simultaneously. One of the most popular and powerful version control systems is Git, which operates on the principle of distributed version control. Let's break down the concepts of local and remote repositories and understand why Git has become immensely popular.

Local Versus Remote Repositories

In its vast ecosystem, Git primarily classifies its storage into two types of repositories: local and remote.

Local Repository

The term '*local repository*' is quite self-explanatory. It's that part of Git that lives and breathes on your own computer or laptop. Think of it as your sandbox, a safe space where you can play around, make changes, commit them, and see the entire timeline of your project. It's like having your own private room where you can rearrange the furniture, paint the walls a different color, or even change the entire decor, all without affecting the rest of the house.

Now, let's dive a bit deeper into the benefits of having such a workspace.

Benefits of a Local Repository

- **Flexibility:** Throughout one's career, having a flexible workspace has always been crucial, and with a local repository, that's exactly what one has. The freedom to make changes at one's own speed without worrying about impacting the mainline or other team members is enjoyable. This freedom isn't just for big changes; it also allows for experimentation with new ideas, no matter how radical they might be. And if things don't work out, reverting to an earlier state or discarding the changes entirely is easy.
- **Speed:** Having a local repository offers a significant advantage: things happen really fast. Since all your actions take place directly on your computer, there's no waiting for files to go up or come down. Tasks like making commits, looking at logs, or checking differences in your code happen almost instantly. You don't need to rely on outside factors like server response times or internet speed. Everything is readily accessible with a simple click.
- **Safety Net:** In the tech world, mistakes are unavoidable. However, with a local repository in Git, these errors are not the end of the world. Over the years, there have been accidental deletions of crucial pieces of code or changes that, looking back, weren't ideal. However, Git has always provided support in such situations. Every change made is recorded because of its strong tracking system. This means that even if you think you have lost something forever, chances are Git has a record of it, ready for recovery.

Real-Time Example

Think about an artist's life for a moment. Before making beautiful artwork on a clean canvas, they usually practice on a rough piece of paper. This paper is like their playground. They can try different strokes, test colors, and sketch ideas without any worry. It's a place where creativity can flow freely. They can make mistakes, erase them, and start fresh without stressing about ruining the final masterpiece. Similarly, a local repository is like that rough sketchpad for developers. It provides them the freedom to explore, learn, and grow without facing big problems.

In the next section, we will further discuss the concept of remote repositories and how they complement local repositories in the world of Git.

Remote Repository

A remote repository is like an online storage space, usually on famous platforms like GitHub or Bitbucket. This remote spot is where teams, whether comprising just two people or a large group of thousands, come together with their code.

Now, why do we need this?

Imagine this: You are working on a project on your local machine, making frequent changes, saving files, and running tests. All is well until your computer crashes unexpectedly. All your work could be lost in an instant. However, with a remote repository in place, any changes made on your local machine can be 'pushed' to this online storage. Conversely, if your team members have added or altered code, you can 'pull' these updates into your local repository, ensuring you are always in sync.

Over the years, it has been recognized that having a remote repository is not just a luxury but a necessity. It bridges the gap between isolated coding on one's personal machine and the collaborative effort needed in most projects today.

Benefits of a Remote Repository

- **Collaboration:** In today's interconnected world, collaboration is the cornerstone of many successful projects. Throughout our tenure in IT, we have collaborated with numerous teams spanning different time zones, and remarkably, seamless collaboration has been a consistent outcome. The remote repository allows for this. No matter where you are, you can contribute to a project, make changes, and ensure that everyone has the latest version of the code. It's like a round-the-clock relay race, where the baton, in this case, the code, is passed smoothly from one contributor to another, leading to a product that has had multiple expert touches.
- **Backup:** In the early years, facing a tough situation due to losing a lot of code because of a hardware problem highlighted how crucial it is to regularly back up your work. With a remote repository, each change you make is securely stored on a cloud server. So, even if your laptop encounters an unfortunate event like a coffee spill or a sudden crash, your weeks or months of hard work remain safe and can be easily recovered.

- **Visibility:** Clear communication is highly value in the IT field. Platforms like GitHub have made coding accessible, allowing not only your team but the worldwide developer community to see your work. This openness creates a feeling of community and shared learning. There have been instances where developers from various places gave feedback or suggested improvements to code. These interactions enhance the coding experience and offer new perspectives.
- **Version Control:** Having a structured version history is like having a detailed journal of your project. In earlier projects, whenever a bug appeared or a feature didn't work as intended, the version history came to the rescue. By looking at the systematic record of changes, we could pinpoint the origin of issues and decide whether to fix them or revert to a previous, stable version.

Real-Time Example

Consider a scenario where a diverse team collaborates on a significant project, comparable to constructing a building. Each team member, representing different roles such as architects, masons, and interior designers, contributes to the project independently. However, to ensure seamless integration of individual efforts, the team regularly updates a remote repository. This collaborative approach guarantees that the project evolves cohesively, resulting in a robust, aesthetic, and functional outcome.

Dual Repository System

In many years of experience working in IT, one of the common challenges observed in software development is managing code changes, especially when multiple people are involved. One might ask, "*Why not just have one place where everyone makes their updates?*" However, having both local and remote repositories is beneficial for the following reasons:

Think about the numerous times you have participated in a group project. If everyone was updating the same shared document or codebase simultaneously, you would have noticed that managing the overlapping changes was a nightmare. The situation is quite similar in software development. When multiple developers try to edit the same file or feature simultaneously, without a structured system in place, the results can be destructive. There have been instances where projects are delayed or even fail because of this chaos.

The dual repository system is Git's answer to this dilemma. It lets each developer have their sandbox, which is their local repository. Here, they can make, test, and even redo their changes without affecting the main codebase. Once they are confident in their updates, they can then push these changes to the remote repository.

Order from Chaos

Over the years in IT, the teams have been seen to struggle with unstructured code management. More often than not, when everyone has access to a shared space, unintentional overwrites happen. For instance, I recall an incident in my career where two of my colleagues made significant changes to the same feature. Without a proper system in place, one person's work was completely overwritten by other's. Hours of effort were lost in a matter of seconds.

With Git's dual repository approach, each contributor has their own dedicated local space. They can experiment, code, and test without the fear of disrupting the main project. Once they are ready, they push their updates to the remote repository. This way, Git ensures that the main codebase remains streamlined and chaos-free.

Review Mechanism

Ensuring the quality of software is crucial in development, and Git plays a role by providing a review process. Before applying any changes from the local repository to the remote one, team members can check it.

There was a project where a junior developer was eager to push his changes. Without reviewing, he would have introduced a major bug into the application. Thankfully, because of Git's review mechanism, a senior developer caught this mistake in time. This not only ensures that the code is error-free but also maintains a consistent coding standard throughout the project.

Parallel Workstreams

One significant advantage of Git is that it lets team members work on different tasks simultaneously. Whether it's adding new features, fixing bugs, or trying out experimental ideas, everyone can work at the same time.

In one of the larger teams I was part of, we were developing an application with multiple modules. With Git, each developer took ownership of a module, working on it independently. Once completed, they merged their work with the main codebase. This ensured that no two developers stepped on each other's toes, and the development process was smooth.

Real-Time Example

Imagine this scenario: a group of writers is working together on a book. If they all write directly into one document, the content would be messy, with overlapping ideas. Instead, each writer creates their chapter separately, polishes it, and then comes together to compile the book. This is similar to how Git's local and remote repositories function.

After years of using different version control systems, the approach of Git, with its two repositories, is considered very effective. It's like the two wheels of a bicycle. Each wheel, or repository, has a specific job. However, it's when they work together that they drive the whole project forward smoothly.

In the following sections, we will explore how to get the most out of these repositories, ensuring a straightforward and productive coding experience.

Now, let's go ahead and create a local Git repository!

Creating Your First Git Repository

As you know, we use Git to manage our project. To begin, you first need to create a Git repository. This is where Git will store and manage all the project-related files, allowing you to track your progress and collaborate with others on your team.

To create a Git repository, you need to run command called `git init` in your Terminal or Git Bash. To do that, open your Git Bash terminal. To confirm your current directory, which is essential for ensuring you initialize the Git repository in the correct location, type the command `pwd` (print working directory). This step is crucial as it helps you verify that you are in the desired directory where you want to set up the Git repository before proceeding with the initialization.

Let's see the output of command `pwd` in Terminal:

```
PravinMishra@Pravin-MacBook-Pro~ pwd
/Users/pravinkumar/workspace
PravinMishra@Pravin-MacBook-Pro~
```

Figure 3.1: *Run command "pwd"*

The PWD command provides information about the current directory. In `pravinkumar` user `workspace` directory, we will create a new project folder using the command `mkdir`. Please ensure that you follow the steps along to avoid getting stuck in later chapters.

Now, let's create `TheCloud_Advisory` project directory. To do this, let us use command `mkdir TheCloud_Advisory`.

Let's see the output of command `mkdir` in Terminal:

```
PravinMishra@Pravin-MacBook-Pro~ mkdir TheCloud_Advisory
PravinMishra@Pravin-MacBook-Pro~
```

Figure 3.2: *Make a directory "The Cloud_Advisory"*

Currently, it is simply a folder in our system. If we make any changes to this folder or a file within it, we will not be able to track or manage those changes. That's the fundamental difference between a directory and a Git repository. To control and track the versions of the files inside a directory, we need to convert it into a Git repository. Let's go ahead and convert the directory `TheCloud_Advisory` into a Git repository. To do that, we use the command **`git init`**. Now, press Enter.

Let's see the output of the Command `git init` in the Terminal:

```
PravinMishra@Pravin-MacBook-Pro~ mkdir TheCloud_Advisory
PravinMishra@Pravin-MacBook-Pro~ cd TheCloud_Advisory
PravinMishra@Pravin-MacBook-Pro~ git init
Initialized empty Git repository in /Users/pravinkumar/workspace/TheCloud_Advisory/.git/
PravinMishra@Pravin-MacBook-Pro~
```

***Figure 3.3**: Run the command "git init"*

We have successfully converted our `TheCloud_Advisory` directory into a Git repository.

As you can see, this repository is currently empty. We can check this by using the command `LS`.

Let's see the output of the command `ls` in the Terminal:

```
PravinMishra@Pravin-MacBook-Pro ~ ls
PravinMishra@Pravin-MacBook-Pro ~
```

***Figure 3.4**: Run command "ls"*

It will show us that there is nothing inside this repository.

Before we move any further, let's understand how **`git init`** converted this directory into a repository.

`git init` created a hidden folder called **`.git`**. This folder is what makes this directory a Git repository. It stores all the information and changes that you make in your files, and Git uses this saved information to manage your files.

Now, let's use the command `ls -a`. It will show us a hidden folder named **`.git`**.

Let's see the output of the command `ls -a` in the Terminal:

```
PravinMishra@Pravin-MacBook-Pro ~ ls -a
.       ..      .git
PravinMishra@Pravin-MacBook-Pro ~
```

***Figure 3.5**: Run command "ls -a"*

This file contains all the information about the other files in the repository that can be tracked by Git. **`.git`** is a default directory structure, and we don't need to change anything in it.

So, from this point on, Git will track any changes you make to the files in the `TheCloud_advisory` folder, and you can start using Git commands like **`git status`**, **`git add`**, **`git`** `commit`, and `git push` to manage your project and collaborate with others on your team. Don't worry, all these commands will be covered in detail in upcoming chapters.

Let's see the output of the command `git status` in the Terminal:

```
PravinMishra@Pravin-MacBook-Pro~ git status
On branch main

No commits yet

nothing to commit (create/copy files and use "git add" to track)
PravinMishra@Pravin-MacBook-Pro~
```

***Figure 3.6**: Run the command "git status"*

When we run **`git status`** in a Git-enabled project directory, the command returns a message stating:

- **On branch main:** This confirms that we are currently on the main branch, which is the default primary branch for any new Git repository. Git branch will be covered in detail in the upcoming chapter.
- **No commits yet:** This line indicates that our repository is freshly initialized and does not yet have any commit history. Commits are snapshots or records of our project at a specific point in time.
- **Nothing to commit (create/copy files and use "git add" to track):** Since this is a new repository, Git is notifying us that there are no files present to commit. To begin versioning our project with Git, we need to create new files or copy existing ones into this directory. Once files are added, we will use the `git add` command to begin tracking them with Git.

Let's see the output of the command `git add` in the Terminal:

```
PravinMishra@Pravin-MacBook-Pro~ git add
Nothing specified, nothing added.
hint: Maybe you wanted to say 'git add .'?
hint: Turn this message off by running
hint: "git config advice.addEmptyPathspec false"
PravinMishra@Pravin-MacBook-Pro~
```

***Figure 3.7**: Run the command "git add"*

The `git add` output indicates that the `git add` command was executed without any arguments. Git expects a file name, a directory, or a pattern to follow after git add. Since nothing was specified and we know there is no file, Git did not add anything to the staging area. The staging area is where Git tracks changes to files before they are committed.

We will learn all these commands in the upcoming chapters. But before that, we need to learn how to configure Git and how to create a file in a Git repository.

Now, let's understand why exactly we need `git config` and what its purpose is.

Git config

`git config` is a Git command used to configure Git on your local computer. It allows you to set your personal information, such as your name and email address. The information is used to identify you as the author of a commit. A commit represents the current changes. Whenever you make changes to your code and save them, each change is identified as a "commit".

Whenever we make a change or attempt a commit, Git tracks:

- Who made the commit?
- When was it made?
- What changes were made?
- Why was the change made?

To ensure that we keep track of everyone who is contributing to our project, we set up our name and email using the command `git config`.

For example, `TheCloud_Advisory` project that we created, there are going to be other developers working on it. All the developers will need to save their information using the `git config` command before they start working on the code. Once everyone's information is saved, it becomes easier for other developers to review and understand the changes made by each developer, and it also helps avoid confusion and potential conflicts.

In simple words, `git config` is like the sign-up form to set up your account in Git so that your contributions to a project can be properly tracked and attributed to you.

Let us now configure Git. There are two types of configurations in Git.

You can configure your details for a single Git repository, which means you will be authorized to make changes in that particular repository. If you attempt to make changes to any other repository, you will have to configure it again. Another type of Git configuration is known as global configuration. As the name suggests, configuring Git globally means you will not have to provide your details for each repository separately. With a single configuration, you will be able to work on all available repositories. So, let's configure Git.

First, you will configure your details for a repository:

To configure your details for a single repository, you can use the git config command with the `--local flag` and pass your details, including your name and email ID. Before we set name and email, let's check the output of the following command.

Enter this code: `git config --local user. name`

Let's see the output in the Terminal:

```
PravinMishra@Pravin-MacBook-Pro~ git config --local user.name

PravinMishra@Pravin-MacBook-Pro~
```

Figure 3.8: *Run the command "git config --local user.name"*

The terminal does not show any output following the command. This typically means that no user.name has been set for this local repository. In Git, if a configuration command is run without a value and the configuration key is not set, Git simply returns with no output.

To set the user.name configuration for the repository, you would follow the git config command with a value, as follows:

```
git config --local user.name "Your Name"
```

Let's see the output in the Terminal:

```
PravinMishra@Pravin-MacBook-Pro~ git config --local user.name "Pravin Mishra"
PravinMishra@Pravin-MacBook-Pro~ git config --local user.name
Pravin Mishra
PravinMishra@Pravin-MacBook-Pro~
```

Figure 3.9: *Run the command "git config --local user.email "Your Name""*

After running this command, the name `Your Name` will be associated with all commits you make in that repository. When you run `git config --local user.name` again, it will output the name you have set.

In a source code management environment, this allows other contributors/developers to see who has made what specific changes. When you make a change, Git records them along with your name and email as the author, which is why it's important to set this up before starting to work on a project.

Now, let's move on and add your email address with the following command:

```
git config --local user.email "youremail@example.com"
```

This command sets the local Git repository's configuration for the user's email address to `"hello@pravinmishra.in"`. The `--local` flag means this email will be used to identify you as the author of commits in this specific repository.

In case you don't use the `--local` flag, as in the following example, it will configure your details for a single repository. It means even if you don't use the `--local flag,` it will function as a local flag only:

```
git config user.name <name>
git config user.email <email id>
```

This will set your name and email address for the current repository only. If you work on multiple repositories, you will need to set your details separately for each repository.

You can also check whether you have successfully configured or not using the command- `git config --user. name`, as shown in *Figure* 3.10:

```
PravinMishra@Pravin-MacBook-Pro~ git config --local user.email "hello@pravinmishra.in"
PravinMishra@Pravin-MacBook-Pro~ git config --local user.email
hello@pravinmishra.in
PravinMishra@Pravin-MacBook-Pro~
```

***Figure* 3.10**: *To verify, run the command "git config --user.email"*

You should see your email in the output, indicating that we have successfully configured it.

Next, let's move on and set up Git configuration on a more universal level with global settings. Using the `--global flag` will apply your configurations across all your repositories on your machine.

To configure your username globally, enter the following command:

```
git config --global user.name "Your Name"
```

```
PravinMishra@Pravin-MacBook-Pro ~ git config --global user.name "name"
PravinMishra@Pravin-MacBook-Pro ~ git config --global user.name "Pravin_Mishra"
PravinMishra@Pravin-MacBook-Pro ~
```

***Figure* 3.11**: *Insert a command "git config --global user.name " name""*

Upon executing this command in your terminal, Git won't output a message, but the name `Your Name` is now set for every action you take within Git on your computer.

Similarly, to set your email address globally, use the following command:

```
"git config --global user.email "email id""
```

Let's see the output in the Terminal:

```
PravinMishra@Pravin-MacBook-Pro ~ git config --global user.email "email id"
PravinMishra@Pravin-MacBook-Pro ~ git config --global user.email "hello@pravinmi
shra.in"
```

***Figure* 3.12**: *Run a command "git config --global user.email "email id""*

After running this command, your email address will be associated with your commits in any repository you work on.

So the `--global flag` sets your details globally, meaning that Git will use these details for all repositories on your computer. This can save you time and effort because you won't have to provide your details for each repository separately.

Please note that if you set your details globally, they will overwrite any local configurations you may have set for individual repositories. So, if you want to use different details for a specific repository, you will need to set them using the `--local flag`.

You can again check whether you have successfully configured or not using the following command:

```
git config --global user. name.
```

Let's see the output in the Terminal:

```
PravinMishra@Pravin-MacBook-Pro~ git config --global user.name
Pravin Mishra
PravinMishra@Pravin-MacBook-Pro~
```

Figure 3.13: *Run a command "git config --global user.email "email id""*

The output should display your name, indicating that you have successfully configured it.

The configured properties in the Terminal are shown in *Figure* 3.14 as follows:

```
PravinMishra@Pravin-MacBook-Pro ~ %git config --list
credential.helper=osxkeychain
init.defaultbranch=main
user.name=Pravin_Mishra
user.email=hello@pravinmishra.in
```

Figure 3.14: *List of configured properties*

Creating a File Inside the Git Repository

Now that you have successfully initialized a Git repository and configured your details, it means if you add any file inside your Git repository, you can track changes made to that file. Let's test all this by creating a file inside the Git repository.

To create a file in the terminal, you can use the touch command followed by the name of the file you want to create. Let us create a file named index.html. So, let us use the following command:

Open the terminal and write the command - touch <index.html>, and press *Enter*.

Let's see the output in the Terminal:

```
PravinMishra@Pravin-MacBook-Pro ~ touch index.html
PravinMishra@Pravin-MacBook-Pro ~
```

Figure 3.15: *Run the command "touch index.html"*

This will create a new file named `index.html` in your Git repository. You can verify that the file was created by using the `ls` command, which lists the files and directories in the current directory:

Let's input the `ls` command in the terminal and press Enter.

Let's see the output in the Terminal:

```
PravinMishra@Pravin-MacBook-Pro~ ls
index.html
PravinMishra@Pravin-MacBook-Pro~ █
```

***Figure 3.16**: Run the command "ls"*

Here, you can see that `index.html` has been created successfully.

Now, you can use any editor to edit and write code in your file. Here, we are using the VS code editor to write the code.

Now, locate the folder where we initiated our Git repository. In this folder, you can see our `index.html` file.

Let's write the HTML code in our `index.html`.

Once you have finished writing the code, return to Git Bash. Writing code in your file is like making changes, and since the file is present in the Git repository, all the changes should be tracked and saved.

Let's go ahead and check that all changes are saved. You can do this by checking the status of your Git repository. For that, use a command called `git status`. Go to Git Bash and enter the command `git status`, and you will see the status of your Git repository.

Let's see the output in the Terminal:

```
PravinMishra@Pravin-MacBook-Pro~ git status
On branch main

No commits yet

Untracked files:
  (use "git add <file>..." to include in what will be committed)
        index.html

nothing added to commit but untracked files present (use "git add" to track)
PravinMishra@Pravin-MacBook-Pro~ █
```

***Figure 3.17**: Run the command "git status"*

Conclusion

In this chapter, we explored the concept of Git repositories, differentiating between local and remote repositories, and walked through the steps of creating and working with them. Repositories play a crucial role in Git, and gaining a solid understanding of them sets the stage for more advanced topics. In our upcoming chapter, we will dive into the essential commands of Git and learn how they interact with repositories to facilitate smooth version control.

CHAPTER 4
Basic Git Commands

Introduction

In this chapter, we will look into the essential tools and commands that form the backbone of working with Git. We will start with the basics, such as checking the status of your repository, tracking changes, and committing those changes. Then, we will explore viewing your Git history, and look into some common operations that are important to managing Git repositories. Additionally, this chapter includes some of the best practices for committing, and tips to avoid its common pitfalls. By the end of this chapter, you will not only be equipped with the key commands to work effectively with Git but also ready to tackle more complex Git operations with confidence.

Let us begin this exciting journey into the world of Git!

Structure

In this chapter, we will cover the following topics:

- Understanding Git Commands
    - Checking the Status of Your Repository Using Git Status
    - Adding Changes to Be Tracked with Git Add
    - Making and Documenting Changes Using Git Commit
    - Viewing Your Git History with Git Log
- Common Operations in Git Repositories
- Best Practices When Committing
- Avoiding Common Pitfalls

By the end of this chapter, you will be well educated to manage your code changes and understand version control better.

Understanding Git Commands

In the previous chapter, we learnt about `git config`, successfully set up our details such as name and email ID, and also created a file inside our Git repository. Now, we are going to learn some important commands of Git.

Let us start with the first command, which is `git status` (as shown in *Figure 4.1*):

```
PravinMishra@Pravin-MacBook-Pro~ git status
On branch main

No commits yet

Untracked files:
  (use "git add <file>..." to include in what will be committed)
        index.html

nothing added to commit but untracked files present (use "git add" to track)
PravinMishra@Pravin-MacBook-Pro~
```

Figure 4.1: *Output of the command git status*

As we see, there is the untracked file `index.html`. Untracked files are those that Git has not been told to keep an eye on, usually new files that have been added to the directory, but not yet added to Git's version control.

Now, let us understand this in detail.

Git Status

`git status` is a command used to get the current status of our local Git repository. It displays information such as when a new file is added, or any changes made to any file. Moreover, it also gives information about whether the file you are working on is saved or not.

Let us understand this with an example.

Assume that you are working on a website, and you have a repository with all the related files. You have been working on the HTML file, but you are not sure whether you have saved all the changes or not.

To check this, just type `git status` (as shown in *Figure* 4.2) into your terminal. If you have added any new file to your repository, it will tell you that a new file is added to the repository, and that it is an untracked file, because you have not saved that file. If you make changes to a file, which is already present in your repository, then it will show that particular file as modified, and you will have to save it again:

```
PravinMishra@Pravin-MacBook-Pro ~ %git status
On branch main
Your branch is up to date with 'origin/main'.

Untracked files:
  (use "git add <file>..." to include in what will be committed)
        index.html

nothing added to commit but untracked files present (use "git add" to track)
PravinMishra@Pravin-MacBook-Pro ~ %
```

Figure 4.2: *Output of the git status command*

This is helpful because it lets you know which files you have been working on, and if any changes still need to be saved, which you can then do. It is like having a checklist that helps you keep track of your work and make sure that everything is up to date and saved.

Now, let us use this command and see what output we are getting.

In the previous chapter, we created an index.html file in the `TheCloud_Advisory` repository, and also wrote some code into the index.html file.

Now, go to the Git bash terminal and type `git status` in the terminal, and press *Enter*. You will be able to see that the output (*Figure* 4.2) reflects the status that we are in the main branch (we will discuss the branch in detail in the next chapter), and you will see that there is one untracked file named index.html. This means that the file which we have created is available in our repository, but we cannot track that file yet.

An untracked file is a file that exists in the working directory, but has not yet been saved to the Git repository. When a file is untracked, Git is not aware of its existence, and therefore does not track any changes made to the file.

To track this file, we first have to add it to the staging area, and then commit changes, which means saving our changes to the repository. We will learn about commits later in the chapter.

When working on our project, we may add some files and edit them, but for Git to track those files and save them, we need to add these files to the staging area once we are done making changes.

Staging area is the area where we save the files with all our changes before the final commit. The files which are available in the staging area are ready to be committed.

We can add files to the staging area with the help of the command `git add`, which we are going to learn about next.

To summarize, with the help of `git status`, we can figure out which files have been added but are not yet tracked by Git, what files have been modified since the last commit, and what files are ready to be committed. It also shows us any other important information, such as the current branch that is open.

By using `git status`, we can quickly see what changes we have made to our code and files, and what we need to do to commit those changes to our repository. This helps us keep track of our work, and ensures that we do not lose any important changes that we have made.

Git Add

`git add` is a command that allows you to add changes made to files in your project to the Git staging area.

Have you ever made changes to a file in your local repository and wondered how to save those changes to Git? While Git does not automatically track changes, it is easy to do so with Git's "`add`" command.

Let us say you are working on a website, and you want to make some changes to the homepage. You open up the `index.html` file and make some changes to the text and images on the page. Now, you want to save those changes to Git. To do this, you would use the `git add` command to add the `index.html` file to the staging area.

The staging area is like a holding area for changes you want to commit to Git.

Think of it like preparing a package for shipping. You gather all the items you want to send, put them in a box, and label it. The staging area is like your box, and the `git add` command is like putting items in that box and labelling it for shipment.

Now, let us add the file by using the command `git add`, as shown in *Figure 4.3a*:

```
nothing added to commit but untracked files present (use "git add" to track)
PravinMishra@Pravin-MacBook-Pro ~ git add
Nothing specified, nothing added.
hint: Maybe you wanted to say 'git add .'?
hint: Turn this message off by running
hint: "git config advice.addEmptyPathspec false"
PravinMishra@Pravin-MacBook-Pro ~ git add index.html
PravinMishra@Pravin-MacBook-Pro ~
```

***Figure 4.3a**: Output of the "**git add**" command*

Let us check the status using `git status` again, as shown in *Figure 4.3b*:

```
PravinMishra@Pravin-MacBook-Pro ~ %git add index.html
PravinMishra@Pravin-MacBook-Pro ~ %git status
On branch main
Your branch is up to date with 'origin/main'.

Changes to be committed:
  (use "git restore --staged <file>..." to unstage)
        new file:   index.html

PravinMishra@Pravin-MacBook-Pro ~ %
```

***Figure 4.3b**: Checking the added file*

In the updated status, you see that the previously untracked file has now been moved to the staging area, assured for the next step in the Git workflow.

By using the `git add` command, we have informed Git about the files we intend to include in our next commit. This staging area acts as a pre-commit holding ground, allowing us to review and finalize our changes before they are permanently recorded in the repository's history.

With our file now staged, we are set to solidify our changes. This is where `git commit` comes into play. `git commit` is the command we use to capture a snapshot of the project's currently staged changes.

In the forthcoming section, we will go deeper into the `git commit` command, learning how to effectively record our project's progress and create a robust version history.

Let us now study `git commit` in detail.

Git Commit

When the changes you made are added in the staging area, it means the changes are ready to be saved permanently in the Git repository. That is where we use `git commit`.

`git commit` is the command that you use to permanently save your changes to the Git repository.

Now, let us understand `git commit`. When you make changes to your code in a Git repository, those changes are not automatically saved as a permanent part of your project history. Instead, you need to run the `git commit` command to save them, followed by a message that describes the changes you have made. This message helps you and others understand what changes were made, and why they were made. It is like writing a thank you note to yourself for a job well done!

Let us understand `git commit` with the help of the previous example.

Let us say you are working on a website, and you want to make some changes to the homepage. You open up the `index.html` file, and make some changes to the text and add new images on the page. You then used the `git add` command to save those changes to the staging area. Once you have staged your changes, you are ready to commit them to Git. To do this, you would use the `git commit` command (as shown in *Figure* 4.4) with a message that describes the changes you have made.

```
"git commit -m "updated the homepage"
```

```
PravinMishra@Pravin-MacBook-Pro ~ Git commit -m updated index.html
[main (root-commit) e6f182f] updated
 1 file changed, 14 insertions(+)
 create mode 100644 index.html
PravinMishra@Pravin-MacBook-Pro ~
```

Figure 4.4: *Output of the command "git commit -m "updated index.html"*

This message tells Git that you have made changes to the files, and at the same time, explains what those changes are. The `-m` flag tells Git that the message is coming next.

After running the `git commit` command, Git will create a new commit in its history, with your changes. This commit will be recorded with a unique identifier. It is like a unique identity number of the commit that you can use to find and refer to it later.

Using `git commit` is important because it allows you to keep track of the changes you have made to your project. You can look back through the commit history to see what changes were made, when they were made, and why. This is especially helpful when working on large projects, or collaborating with others, as it helps everyone stay on the same page.

In simple words, commit means saving the changes in our local Git repository. We can commit our changes with the help of the `git commit` command, and it will save our work in the local Git repository.

We can also check the history of our commit using a `git log` command, which we are going to learn in the next section.

Git Log

Suppose you are working on a project, and you made multiple commits in your project. Now, you want to check the history of your commits. This is where "`git log`" comes into the picture:

```
PravinMishra@Pravin-MacBook-Pro ~ git log
commit e6f182f570a40c52cc6d35816e3f1ce36d957dcd (HEAD -> main)
Author: Pravin Mishra <hello@pravinmishra.in>
Date:   Sat Nov 18 12:45:51 2023 +0530

    updated
PravinMishra@Pravin-MacBook-Pro ~
```

Figure 4.5: *Output of the command "git log"*

`git log` is a command used in the Git version control system to view the history of changes made to your repository. When you run this command, Git will display a list of commits with the most recent commit appearing first (refer to *Figure* 4.5).

Each commit in the list will show you information such as the commit hash, which is a unique identifier for the commit, the author of the commit, the date and time at which the commit was made, and the message saved in the commit.

Let us understand this with the help of the same example of the website.

Suppose you are working on a website. You have made several commits to the repository, and now you want to see the history of those commits.

To view the commit history, you will type in the command `git log` in the terminal, and press *Enter*.

Then, in the output, you will see that there are multiple commits in the repository, listed with the most recent commit first. Each commit is identified by a unique hash, followed by the name and email ID of the author of the commit, the date and time it was made, and the commit message describing the changes made in that commit.

`git log` helps keep track of changes made to your source code, understanding who made the changes, and when.

Let us check the history of our repository.

Open the Terminal and enter the command `git log`, and press *Enter*.

Now, you can see the logs. As of now, we have only done one commit, so it is showing us that one commit.

It also shows details such as who the author of the commit is, and the date and time of when the commit was made.

You will also notice that it gives a commit hash, which is a unique identifier for the commit. We will see where this commit hash will be useful in the subsequent chapter.

Let us update the file `index.html` (refer to *Figure* 4.6):

```
<p style="color:red;font-size:294%;"><i><b> This is a paragraph. </b></i></p>

<h2 style="color:pink;">This is heading 8</h2>

<h3 style="color:green;font-size:200%;">This is heading 35</h3>

<h4 style="color:orange;">This is heading 4</h4>

<h5 style="color:brown;">This is heading 5</h5>

<h6 style="color:coral;">This is heading 6</h6>

</body>
</html>
~
~
~
~
~
~
~
~
~
```

Figure 4.6: *Updated file index.html*

We will open the **VS code** and make some changes.

After we have updated the file `index.html`, let us go back to the Git bash.

Now, let us check the status using `git status` (refer to *Figure* 4.7):

```
PravinMishra@Pravin-MacBook-Pro ~ git status
warning: could not open directory '.Trash/': Operation not permitted
On branch main
Changes not staged for commit:
  (use "git add <file>..." to update what will be committed)
  (use "git restore <file>..." to discard changes in working directory)
        modified:   index.html
```

Figure 4.7: *Check the output of the git status command in Terminal*

Here, you can see that the file has been modified. Whenever we modify any file in the repository, we have to commit changes, and before commit, we need to stage the changes.

As you can see, changes are not staged for commit. Therefore, always remember, whenever we make any changes to our file, we need to stage those changes first, and then commit.

Let us create one more file in our repository with the name of `style.css`.

Go to the Terminal, use the command "`touch style.css`", and press *Enter* (refer to *Figure 4.8*):

```
PravinMishra@Pravin-MacBook-Pro ~ touch style.css
```

Figure 4.8: *Output of file created in Terminal that is "touch style.css"*

Now, use the command `git status` to get the status of our Git repository (refer to *Figure 4.9*):

```
PravinMishra@Pravin-MacBook-Pro~ git status
On branch main

No commits yet

Changes to be committed:
  (use "git rm --cached <file>..." to unstage)
        new file:   index.html

Changes not staged for commit:
  (use "git add <file>..." to update what will be committed)
  (use "git restore <file>..." to discard changes in working directory)
        modified:   index.html

Untracked files:
  (use "git add <file>..." to include in what will be committed)
        style.css

PravinMishra@Pravin-MacBook-Pro~
```

Figure 4.9: *Output of the command git status*

These are the files that have been modified since the last commit, but have not been staged yet.

Now, we see that `index.html` has been modified since it was staged. To include these latest changes, we need to stage the file again using Git add `index.html`. Alternatively, if we decide against keeping these modifications, we can discard them with **`git restore`** `index.html`.

There is also the aspect of untracked files. The `style.css` is untracked as we have created a new file, which means that Git is not keeping track of this file yet. To begin tracking, we should add it to the staging area using `git add style.css`.

If you want to stage all modified and untracked files at once, use the command "git add", which is a convenient way to stage all changes at once. This command is particularly useful when we have multiple files to stage and want to save time by adding them all in a single command rather than one by one (refer to *Figure* 4.10):

```
PravinMishra@Pravin-MacBook-Pro ~ git add .
warning: could not open directory 'Library/Application Support/CallHistoryTransactions/'
: Operation not permitted
```

Figure 4.10: *Status of command "git add"*

Now, enter the command `git add` and press *Enter*, and you can see all the files are staged.

Now, let us commit these changes (refer to *Figure* 4.11):

```
git commit -m "modified index.html and added style.css"
```

```
PravinMishra@Pravin-MacBook-Pro~ git commit -m 'modified index.html and added style.css'
[main (root-commit) 355201f] modified index.html and added style.css
 2 files changed, 10 insertions(+)
 create mode 100644 index.html
 create mode 100644 style.css
PravinMishra@Pravin-MacBook-Pro~
```

Figure 4.11: *Add two files – style.css and index.html*

Now, let us do the Git log once again.

Here, we can see that the latest commit is changed, and now there are two commits – one is the initial commit, and the other is the latest one:

```
PravinMishra@Pravin-MacBook-Pro~ git status
On branch main
nothing to commit, working tree clean
PravinMishra@Pravin-MacBook-Pro~ git log
commit fc938ecce3162b14b0ca3d025a24d5ed452062e6 (HEAD -> main)
Author: Pravin Mishra <hello@pravinmishra.in>
Date:   Tue Mar 12 05:09:03 2024 +0200

    added style.css

commit 355201f052e824eaeb24a544daaff86023834de9
Author: Pravin Mishra <hello@pravinmishra.in>
Date:   Tue Mar 12 05:02:14 2024 +0200

    modified index.html and added style.css
PravinMishra@Pravin-MacBook-Pro~
```

Figure 4 12: *Git log*

This is how we can check the history of our commits using "git log".

Common Operations in Git Repositories

One of the amazing facets of Git is the vast range of operations it offers, allowing seamless collaboration and efficient project management. Understanding the basic operations in Git is very important as they are the core actions you will be performing almost daily when working on any project.

In this section, we will explore each of these operations in depth, illustrating them with real-world scenarios to make them more relatable and understandable.

Clone

`git clone` is the act of creating a local copy of a remote repository, complete with all the branches, tags, and commit history. This operation is similar to downloading a folder from the internet, but provides the full functionality of version control.

Consider this real-time example: You have come across an open-source project on GitHub that piques your interest, and you are keen on contributing. To begin, you need a local version of the project. You can do this by executing:

```
git clone https://github.com/exampleuser/example-repo.git
```

Basically, you are using this command to duplicate *example-repo* onto your machine, of not just the current files, but the entire development history. This cloned repository will include a default remote called origin, pointing back to the source, and by default, the files will be placed in a directory named *example-repo*, unless you specify otherwise.

The clone command is as follows:

```
git clone <repository URL> [<directory>]
```

Let us understand this:

- **<repository URL>**: This is the URL of the repository you wish to clone, which can be found on the repository's GitHub page.
- **[<directory>]**: This is the folder on your local machine where the repository will be cloned into. If not specified, Git uses the repo's name.

After cloning, you might want to move into the project directory, set up your development environment, or switch to a different branch to start your work. The `git clone` command also supports various options, such as `--depth` 1 for a shallow clone, which is useful for saving time and space when history is not a concern.

Figure 4.13 shows the terminal output after running the `git clone` command, where messages indicate the cloning process of each file and branch, concluding with a '`done`' message:

```
PravinMishra@Pravin-MacBook-Pro ~ git clone https://github.com/freeCodeCamp/freeCodeCamp.git
Cloning into 'freeCodeCamp'...
remote: Enumerating objects: 452429, done.
remote: Counting objects: 100% (12738/12738), done.
remote: Compressing objects: 100% (591/591), done.
Receiving objects:  36% (164731/452429), 104.03 MiB | 3.78 MiB/s
```

***Figure 4.13**: Output of the command "git clone"*

Fetch

Git fetch is like receiving a letter in the mail. You have got the information, but you have not read it just yet. In Git, "`git fetch`" is the command that allows you to bring in the latest commits from a remote repository without automatically merging them into your current work. This is important for keeping tabs on changes without disrupting your local development.

Real-Time Example:

Think back to the days of eagerly waiting for your favorite weekly magazine to arrive. You see it at your doorstep and bring it inside, but you may not read it right away. In a similar way, during my early days of collaboration, I often ran `git fetch` multiple times a day. It allowed me to see the landscape of changes others had made – similar to skimming through the magazine's table of contents – without merging those changes into my local branch until I was ready.

Practical Usage:

While `git fetch` alone does not affect your working directory, it is a good practice to run it frequently. It keeps you informed about the project's progress without altering your in-progress work. For a closer look at the fetched changes, use `git log` or `git diff` in conjunction with `git fetch`. This combination provides a powerful way to review what has happened upstream before you decide to merge those changes.

By fetching regularly, you stay up to date with what others are doing, and can prepare your work for seamless integration, avoiding the big interruptions that can come from sudden, unexpected changes.

Command:

```
git fetch origin
```

This command will update your local copy of the remote repository's branches. After fetching, you can examine the updates using `git log origin/<branch-name>` to review the incoming commits, or `git diff origin/<branch-name>` to see the code changes before integrating them with a merge.

Pull

Git pull is the next logical step after fetching in the Git workflow. If fetch is similar to receiving a letter, the pull is not only receiving it but also opening and reading the contents. In Git terms, `git pull` executes two fundamental operations: it fetches changes from a remote repository and then immediately merges them into your current local branch.

Real-Time Example:

Imagine subscribing to an online newsletter rather than a magazine. As soon as a new edition is published, it arrives in your email inbox, and you read it immediately to stay informed. In a software development scenario, I have encountered times when my local branch fell behind the main repository, leading to complications during integration. To mitigate this, I made it a practice to regularly execute Git pull, which kept my local branch up-to-date and in sync with the central codebase, thus preventing many potential issues and ensuring a smoother workflow.

Detailed Operation:

When you issue a `git pull` command, Git fetches the specified remote branch's latest updates and attempts to merge them into your current branch. It is an important command for collaborative work, as it helps reconcile remote changes with your local development. It is advisable to ensure you are ready to integrate those changes and that your work is at a safe stopping point before you pull, to avoid merge conflicts or disruptions in your workflow.

For example, if you are working on a feature branch and need to incorporate updates from the main branch, you will run `git pull origin main`. This command fetches and merges the latest main branch changes into your feature branch, keeping you aligned with the team's collective progress.

Command:

```
git pull origin main
```

By executing the `git pull` (see *Figure* 4.14) command, you ensure that your local main branch is updated with the most recent commits from the origin repository. If there are changes, Git will automatically merge them into your branch:

```
PravinMishra@Pravin-MacBook-Pro ~ git pull
remote: Enumerating objects: 289, done.
remote: Counting objects: 100% (289/289), done.
remote: Compressing objects: 100% (60/60), done.
remote: Total 289 (delta 229), reused 289 (delta 229), pack-reused 0
Receiving objects: 100% (289/289), 128.00 KiB | 2.06 MiB/s, done.
Resolving deltas: 100% (229/229), completed with 82 local objects.
From https://github.com/freeCodeCamp/freeCodeCamp
 + 9c36033dce...e2ce8e1001 i18n-sync-curriculum -> origin/i18n-sync-curriculum  (forced update)
Already up to date.
```

***Figure 4.14**: Output of the command "git pull"*

Push

The "`git push`" command is the grand finale of the work in your local repository. It is when your changes are made final. The command uploads your committed changes to a remote repository. So, you share your progress with the team and integrate your work into the larger project.

Real-Time Example:

Imagine you and your colleagues are co-authors writing a novel. Each of you works on different chapters or sections. When you finish writing and refining your chapter, you need to make it available to your co-authors and readers. In the case of Git, `git push` is how you publish your work. You have completed your edits on your local machine, and with `git push`, your chapter is now live in the remote repository. Your collaborators can immediately access your latest contributions and continue the story, enhancing the narrative with their own additions.

Detailed Operation:

When you issue the Git push command, you are initiating a transfer of your local branch's commits to the remote repository. It is important to have committed all your changes first, as `git push` does not send your working directory or staged changes, only your commits.

Before pushing, it is also a good practice to `git pull` and merge any upstream changes to avoid conflicts. This ensures that your push will be a smooth upload rather than a disruptive force in the project.

Command:

```
git push origin feature-branch
```

Here, you are specifically pushing your feature branch to the origin remote. It is likely your project is hosted on GitHub or another remote server. It makes your latest commits available to the rest, updating the remote repository's state with your local developments.

Checking Status

The `git status` command has been my trusty companion. It provides a snapshot of your current repository, showing which files have changes, which are staged, and which are yet to be staged.

Real-Time Example:

Let us take the example of the daily routine of checking your phone for new messages, missed calls, or updates. As we know, each notification provides a cue for action. In the collaborative environment of software development, `git status` offers a similar snapshot, but of your repository. It shows which files have been modified or staged, and which are still waiting for your attention. This command is helpful in ensuring that no file is left behind before moving forward with commits, pushes, or pulls, especially when multiple team members contribute code simultaneously.

Command:

```
git status
```

When you input the `git status` (see *Figure* 4.15) command, Git responds with a detailed status report. It lists out new untracked files, modifications that have not been staged, and changes that are queued up for the next commit. This visibility is vital in managing a well-organized and up-to-date repository:

```
PravinMishra@Pravin-MacBook-Pro~ git status
On branch main
Changes not staged for commit:
  (use "git add <file>..." to update what will be committed)
  (use "git restore <file>..." to discard changes in working directory)
        modified:   index.html
        modified:   style.css

Untracked files:
  (use "git add <file>..." to include in what will be committed)
        main.js

no changes added to commit (use "git add" and/or "git commit -a")
PravinMishra@Pravin-MacBook-Pro~
```

***Figure* 4.15**: *Output of the command git status*

Figure 4.15 shows a list that categorizes the state of files in your working directory and staging area. For example, it might highlight files that are "*modified but not staged*" or "*staged but not yet committed*," allowing you to determine your next actions with clarity.

Best Practices When Committing

Let us now move on to learning one of the most important aspects of using Git effectively, that is, committing its best practices. It has been noticed that newer developers, and even some experienced ones, sometimes overlook the significance of this simple process. However, if done right, it can save you from a lot of headaches down the line.

Frequency of Commits

In the world of Git, in which a variety of methodologies and workflows are implemented, the question of how often to commit is one that frequently arises. Instead of waiting for a large chunk of code or multiple features to be completed, aim for smaller, more frequent commits.

Here are a few reasons for this:

Easier Troubleshooting

If an issue crops up, it is much simpler to trace the origin of the problem with smaller commit chunks. You can quickly identify which particular commit caused the problem, and rectify it. With larger commits, pinpointing the exact line of code or function that led to the issue becomes a tedious process.

Enhanced Collaboration

If you are working with a team, frequent commits ensure that your peers are always updated with the latest changes. This encourages a more collaborative environment where everyone is on the same page.

Efficient Rollbacks

Git is a lifesaver when something goes wrong. Making smaller commits means you can easily go back to a stable state with just one command.

However, if you make a big commit, and something goes wrong, going back would mean losing a lot of work.

Real-Time Example

Consider putting together a big picture. Each part you add is like a step or a small detail in your project. Instead of waiting to add large pieces, you decide to include each part as soon as you find where it fits. This way of working has two main advantages:

- **Immediate Error Detection:** If a block does not fit right, or affects the stability of your structure, you notice it immediately. This immediate feedback allows for swift corrections, without affecting the broader structure.
- **Progress Tracking:** By adding each piece step by step, you can see the structure evolve and grow. This not only gives a sense of accomplishment but also helps in planning the next steps more effectively.

Think about it like regularly saving your work. When you commit often in Git, it is like saving each part of your project step by step. This way, you quickly see what is going well, fix mistakes easily, and keep an eye on how your project is coming together in real-time.

Size of Commits

Many of us often find ourselves rushing through projects, making many changes at once, and then bundling them all together into a single commit. This is a problematic approach, as not only will it make it challenging to identify specific changes later on, but it will also pose a risk. For example, if one part of a large commit is faulty and needs to be reverted, one would be forced to discard other unrelated changes that were perfectly fine.

Everyone should thus appreciate and follow the mantra, "*Each commit should represent a single logical change.*" This is a practice that has saved me countless hours of headaches and confusion.

Benefits:

- **Logical Segmentation:** Like individual beads on a string, each commit represents a distinct facet of the project's evolution. This segmentation helps in pinpointing when a particular change was made.
- **Simplified Troubleshooting:** As each commit serves as isolated changes, identifying the origin of an issue becomes a straightforward task. It allows for selective reversion, removing the bug without losing collateral work.

Descriptive Commit Messages

At first, when you have tight deadlines, or just want your code to work, you might end up writing really simple commit messages, such as "*Fixed bug*" or "*Updated code.*" You might not realize how important it is to have clear and detailed commit messages until you go back to old projects or work with a team.

Suppose a developer was working on a tricky web project with lots of features, from user authentication to showing data. If, while trying to find a tricky bug, they look at the history of changes they made (called *commit history*) and see vague messages , such as "*Updated function*" or "*Fixed issue*", they will have to spend hours, or days, going through each change, trying to figure out what they did. It is frustrating, and makes them rethink how they write committed messages.

The advice is thus to always write clear and helpful commit messages. These messages are not just for you, but for anyone who might work with the code later on. It could be a colleague, someone from a future team, or even the developer coming back to the project after a long break.

Let us look at the importance of a descriptive commit message through an example.

Consider the following command:

```
git commit -m "Fix navigation bar alignment issue on mobile devices"
```

```
PravinMishra@Pravin-MacBook-Pro~ git commit -m "Fix navigation bar alignment
issue on mobile devices"
[main 7636208] Fix navigation bar alignment issue on mobile devices
 3 files changed, 3 insertions(+), 1 deletion(-)
 create mode 100644 main.js
PravinMishra@Pravin-MacBook-Pro~
```

Figure 4.16: *Output of the command "git commit -m "Fix navigation bar alignment issue on mobile devices"*

Think about reviewing the commit history a few months later, or a new team member trying to understand the evolution of the project. When they see a commit message such as this, they will quickly understand what the changes were about ("*Fix navigation bar alignment*"), and why it was needed ("*on mobile devices*"). The message makes it clear and easy to understand the purpose of that commit.

Compare that to a more unclear message such as "*Fixed nav bar*". It leaves many unanswered questions. What was the issue with the navigation bar? Was it a functionality problem, a design problem, or something else? Where did this issue show up – on desktop browsers, mobile devices, or tablets? Without a clear descriptive message, developers are left to make guesses, or, even worse, face more confusion. They have to dig into the code to figure out what is going on.

Writing clear commit messages is a practice that speaks volumes about the professionalism of a developer. It shows respect for the collaborative nature of coding, acknowledging that our work is not done in isolation, but as part of a broader team effort.

Moreover, in a professional environment, especially when working on larger projects or open-source contributions, clear commit messages become essential. They facilitate code reviews, making it easier for reviewers to understand the rationale behind each change. They also help in debugging, allowing developers to quickly identify when a particular issue was introduced.

In conclusion, as you explore the vast landscape of Git and GitHub, it is important to remember the human element behind every line of code and every commit message. By taking an extra minute or two to craft a clear, descriptive message, we not only make our work more understandable but also contribute to a more collaborative and efficient coding environment.

Avoiding Common Pitfalls

While errors can sometimes be frustrating, they often provide the best learning opportunities. In this light, Git offers a multitude of commands to help developers correct their mistakes.

Let us look into some of the use cases and Git commands that will be helpful.

Undoing Local Changes

Imagine that it is late at night, and you are trying to wrap up a feature before the end of the day. You have made a series of changes to a file, only to realize that these changes do not align with the project's requirements. Before you go down the rabbit hole of manually reverting each change, Git provides a straightforward way to help you out with the `git checkout` command.

```
git checkout <filename>
```

When you execute `git checkout <filename>`, Git will perform several operations under the hood to revert the specified file to its last committed state. This command is particularly useful when you want to discard changes made to a file that has not yet been staged or committed.

Correcting a Premature Commit

Another common situation that many developers often find themselves in is committing changes prematurely. Maybe you forgot to add a file, or perhaps you noticed a bug just after committing. In this situation, you can use git reset.

This offers you a way to undo that last commit while retaining your changes in the staging area. It is as if you have pulled your changes back from the brink of being permanently recorded, allowing you the chance to rectify any oversights or add missing pieces before committing again.

`Git reset` will allow you to rest a commit after pushing it to the remote repository. However there are some limitations we must understand.

If you have already pushed the commit to a remote repository, resetting the commit locally is not enough. The remote repository still contains the commit.

Behavior:

When you attempt to push after local reset:

Git will reject the push because the commit history on the remote repository has diverged from your local repository.

Solution:

If you are sure about modifying the commit history, you can force push (`git push -f`) to overwrite the remote branch with your local branch. However, force pushing is risky and can lead to conflicts if others have made changes in the meantime.

Amending the Last Commit:

Instead of resetting, you can use `git commit --amend` to make changes to the last commit and create a new commit.

Instead of panicking or wondering how to correct this, Git has a remedy for this as well (refer to *Figure* 4.17):

Command:

```
git reset --soft HEAD^
```

```
PravinMishra@Pravin-MacBook-Pro ~ git reset --soft HEAD^
PravinMishra@Pravin-MacBook-Pro ~
```

***Figure* 4.17**: *Output of the command "git reset --soft HEAD^"*

The `--soft` option ensures your changes remain in the staging area, indicating that they are ready to be committed again. For those times when you wish to discard the commit and all its associated changes, the `--hard` option comes into play.

Real-Time Example:

Visualize a scenario where you have worked hard on a project report. After reviewing and double-checking, you submit it confidently. However, moments later, you recall a critical detail that you have overlooked. If there was a way, you would want to redo the report, make the necessary corrections, and then resubmit. The `git reset` command does precisely this, giving you a second chance to rectify your oversight.

Amending a Commit

Even with meticulous planning and careful execution, small oversights can occur. Maybe you forgot to include a file in your commit, or misspelled a word in your commit message.

Amending an Older Commit

Amending an older commit involves modifying a commit that is not the latest one. This operation allows you to add or modify changes in a specific commit, even if it is not the most recent commit.

Thankfully, Git has a solution to modify the very last commit you made (refer to *Figure 4.18*).

Command:

```
git commit --amend
```

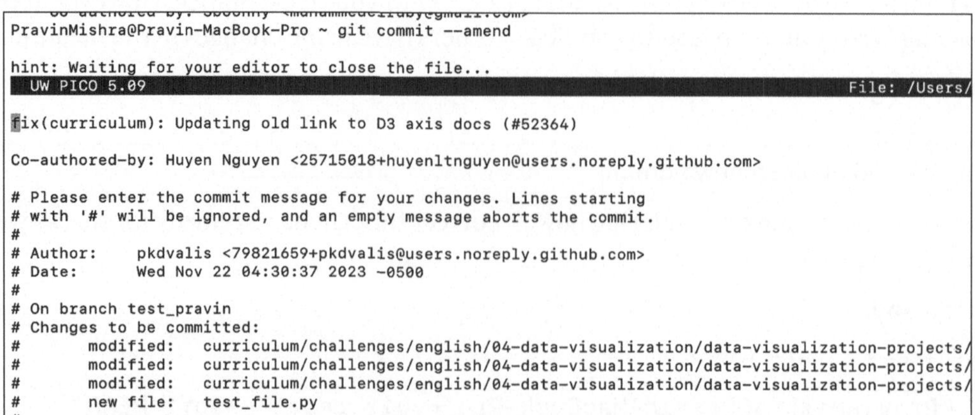

Figure 4.18: *Output of Command "git commit --amend"*

Real-Time Example:

Let us say you have sent out an important document via email. Moments later, you realize a small but significant error in it. If given an opportunity, you would promptly send out a corrected version with a brief note, asking the recipients to disregard the previous version and consider the latest one. The `git commit --amend` command allows you to do just that with your commits. It lets you replace the last commit with a new one that includes any additional changes you have made.

Conclusion

In this chapter, we have journeyed through the core commands that serve as the bedrock for any user's interaction with Git. From assessing the state of your repository using `git status` to tracking changes with `git add`, and solidifying those changes with `git commit`, we have laid down the essential groundwork for managing and documenting your work effectively. The `git log` command has given us a window into the history of our projects, enabling us to reflect on our development journey and understand the evolution of our codebase.

We have also touched upon some common operations that are integral to daily Git use, and discussed the best practices for committing changes. This not only helps in maintaining a clear project history, but also facilitates a smoother workflow for individual developers and teams alike. Additionally, we have explored some typical pitfalls that one might encounter, and provided guidance on how to steer clear of them, ensuring a hassle-free Git experience.

As we turn to the next chapter, "*Branching and Merging: Streamlining Your Development Workflow*," we will build upon this foundational knowledge. You will learn about the powerful branching capabilities of Git, which allow multiple features to be developed in parallel, and how merging can help you seamlessly integrate these features back into the main line of development.

Prepare to dive deeper into the collaborative aspects of Git, understand how to manage your code in a team setting effectively, and begin leveraging the full potential of distributed version control.

CHAPTER 5
Branching and Merging

Introduction

Welcome to the chapter on *Branching and Merging*. In this chapter, we will understand the essential concepts and practical aspects of managing branches and merging changes in your version control workflow. Understanding these fundamental operations is key to efficiently collaborating with others and maintaining a well-organized codebase. Let's explore the ins and outs of branching and merging, keeping it straightforward and accessible for all levels of readers.

Structure

By the end of this chapter, we will have a solid grasp on:

- Git Branching
- Importance of Branches
- Creating a Git Branch
- The `'Git Checkout'` Command
- Combining Work with 'Git Merge'
- Resolving Merge Conflicts
- Best Practices and Common Pitfalls
- Real-World Scenarios and Solutions

Understanding Git Branching

As we understand, **Version Control** is a way to track changes made to code over time. **Git is a popular version control system** that allows developers to work on a project collaboratively and keep track of changes made to the code.

When we say that multiple people can work together in Git without affecting each other's code, then a question may arise: How is this even possible?

The answer to that question is **Git Branch**.

Git branching enables developers to create different versions of the code, which can be worked on and modified independently. This is useful when working on new features or fixing bugs without affecting the main code, which is present in the master branch.

When a Git repository is created, Git generates a default branch named `master`, or you can give the name of your choice, such as main, release, and so on.

Each branch in Git is like a separate copy of the code, allowing modifications without affecting the main code from the master branch. After completing work on a branch, you can merge it back into the main code.

A branch is a version of the code that is separate from the main code present in the default master branch, where you can experiment with changes to your code without affecting the main code.

Branches are useful because they allow you to work on new features, fix bugs, or experiment with different approaches to your code, all without affecting the main code.

Git branching is a powerful tool that allows developers to work on multiple versions of their projects simultaneously, collaborate with others, and track changes to their code over time.

Now, let's understand with an example.

Imagine you are working on a project to create a website with a team of developers. You want to add a new feature to the website but don't want to disrupt the main code while you are working on it.

Using Git branching, you can create a new branch in the Git repository with the command `git branch <new branch name>`. This new branch is like a separate copy of the code that you can work on without affecting the main website. Once you have created the new branch, you can make changes to the code for the new feature.

Meanwhile, when you are working on the new branch, the rest of the team can continue working on the main code without being affected by the changes you are making in the new branch.

Once you have finished working on the new feature, you can merge the changes from the new branch back into the main code. This will add the new feature to the website without disrupting the work that the rest of the team is doing.

If this sounds complicated, don't worry. It will soon become clearer to you.

Overall, Git branching allows you to work on different versions of your website simultaneously, collaborate with others, and track changes to your code over time. This can help you work more efficiently and avoid disrupting the main code while you are working on new features or bug fixes.

If you have any working project with several branches, then go ahead and type the `git branch` command on that project. Your screen will resemble *Figure* 5.1:

```
PravinMishra@Pravin-MacBook-Pro ~ %git branch
  bugfix1
+ bugfix2
  develop
  feature-A
  feature-B
  main
  master
* new-feature
```

***Figure* 5.1:** *Git branch*

Understanding the Importance of Branches

At its core, a branch in Git represents an independent line of development. Think of it as a separate workspace where you can make changes without affecting the main or other branches. This is particularly useful when working on new features or testing out ideas. You can experiment freely, knowing that your main codebase remains untouched.

Using branches ensures that the main code (often referred to as the `master` or `main` branch) remains stable. New features or experiments are worked on separate branches, and only after thorough testing and review are they integrated back into the main codebase.

Creating a Git Branch

Creating a new branch is straightforward. The command you need is as follows:

```
git branch <branch_name>
```

To create a branch named develop, open the terminal and enter the command `git branch develop`, then press *Enter*. This will create a new branch with the name `develop`.

Now, let's understand why we need to create a new branch.

Creating a New Branch

In Git, creating a branch involves diverging from the main line of development to work on a new set of changes, whether it's for implementing a new feature, fixing a bug, or making any other modifications. Let's go into the process of creating a Git branch, where it starts, and why it is essential.

Starting Point of a Branch:

When you create a branch in Git, it originates from a specific commit in the existing branch, typically the main branch (often named master or main). This starting point is known as the **branch point** or **commit reference**. The branch you are creating essentially begins with an identical snapshot of the code at that specific commit.

Now, let's create a develop branch in Git as follows:

```
PravinMishra@Pravin-MacBook-Pro ~ git branch develop
PravinMishra@Pravin-MacBook-Pro ~
```

Figure 5.2: *Output of command "git branch develop"*

Here, you can see that `develop` is successfully created.

Explanation:

This command creates a new branch named `develop` in your Git repository.

The starting point of the branch is crucial because it determines the commit history from which the new branch diverges. The commit where you run the `git branch` command becomes the common ancestor for both the current branch and the newly created `develop` branch.

To check if the branch is successfully created or not, use the command `git branch`; it will list all the branches, as shown in *Figure* 5.3:

```
PravinMishra@Pravin-MacBook-Pro ~ git branch
  Pravin_Cloud
* develop
```

Figure 5.3: *Output of command "git branch"*

Over the years, it has been found beneficial to name branches descriptively. For instance, if you are working on a new login feature, a name like `login-feature` is more descriptive than simply `new branch`. This makes it easier for both you and your teammates to understand the purpose of a branch at a glance.

Now that we have successfully created a new branch, you might be wondering how to access and switch to that branch.

Switch to the New Branch:

After creating the `develop` branch, you typically switch to it to start working on that branch using the `git checkout` command, or more recently, using the `git switch` command.

Now, we have learned how to create a new branch using the `branch <any name>` command. To check whether that branch was created or not, we can use the `git switch` or `git checkout` commands.

So, we can switch from one branch to another with the help of the `git checkout` command. We will discuss this in-depth in the next section.

Git Checkout

As you know, the branch is a copy of your code that exists separately from the main code and allows you to work on changes without affecting the main code. Git checkout is a command that allows you to switch between different branches.

If you have multiple branches for different features of your project, you can use `git checkout` to switch to a specific branch and start working on it.

Alternatively, you can also use `git checkout` to revert to a previous commit or version of your code if you need to undo some changes. Basically, it is used to manage your code or file versions and switch between them whenever needed.

Let's first understand how we can switch between the branches using `git checkout`.

Suppose you are working on a website project that has two branches: `master` and `develop`.

The `master` branch has the main code, while the `develop` branch is used for adding some additional features to the website.

First, you can use the command `git branch` to list all the branches that exist in your repository. In this example, there are two branches, so it will list both branches: master and develop. The asterisk (*) indicates that you are currently on the master branch.

Switching between branches is also simple. To do this, use the following command:

```
git checkout <branch_name>
```

To switch to the `develop` branch, run the command `git checkout develop`.

Before we move into the develop branch, we will see the status of Git using the command `git status`, as shown in *Figure* 5.4:

```
PravinMishra@Pravin-MacBook-Pro ~ %git status
On branch new-feature
Changes not staged for commit:
  (use "git add/rm <file>..." to update what will be committed)
  (use "git restore <file>..." to discard changes in working directory)
        modified:   index.html
        deleted:    pravin.txt

Untracked files:
  (use "git add <file>..." to include in what will be committed)
        pravin_updated.txt

no changes added to commit (use "git add" and/or "git commit -a")
PravinMishra@Pravin-MacBook-Pro ~ %git checkout develop
M       index.html
D       pravin.txt
Switched to branch 'develop'
```

Figure 5.4: *Output of the command "git status"*

Now, you are at the develop branch, as shown in *Figure* 5.5:

```
PravinMishra@Pravin-MacBook-Pro ~ git checkout develop
Switched to branch 'develop'
PravinMishra@Pravin-MacBook-Pro ~ 
```

Figure 5.5: *Output of command "git checkout develop"*

You can now make changes to your code in the `develop` branch, such as adding a new feature or fixing a bug. After completing your changes, you can stage and commit your changes using the `git add` and `git commit` commands.

You can also check the branch name using the command `git branch`, which will show you the available branches in your Git repository.

Go to a terminal and enter the command `git branch`, then press *Enter*. You will see two branches: `master` and `develop`. The asterisk (*) is at `develop`, which means we are on the `develop` branch.

Now, to add styling to our website, create a `style.css` file and add the necessary styling for your website.

Let's see the contents of the `style.css` file, as shown in *Figure* 5.6:

```
PravinMishra@Pravin-MacBook-Pro ~ %cat style.css
body {
  margin: 0;
  font-family: -apple-system, BlinkMacSystemFont, 'Segoe UI', 'Roboto', 'Oxygen',
    'Ubuntu', 'Cantarell', 'Fira Sans', 'Droid Sans', 'Helvetica Neue',
    sans-serif;
  -webkit-font-smoothing: antialiased;
  -moz-osx-font-smoothing: grayscale;
}

code {
  font-family: source-code-pro, Menlo, Monaco, Consolas, 'Courier New',
    monospace;
}
PravinMishra@Pravin-MacBook-Pro ~ %
```

Figure 5.6: *Sample contents of style.css file*

We have added some code to our style.css. After modifying any file in the Git repository, it is necessary to add that file first to the staging area. So, let's return to the terminal and use the command `git add style.css`; it will add the file to the staging area, as shown in *Figure* 5.7:

```
PravinMishra@Pravin-MacBook-Pro ~ git add style.css
PravinMishra@Pravin-MacBook-Pro ~ git status
On branch develop
Changes to be committed:
  (use "git restore --staged <file>..." to unstage)
        modified:   style.css
```

Figure 5.7: *Output of command "git add style.css"*

Now, use the command '`git commit -m "Added more styling"`' and press *Enter* (see *Figure* 5.8):

```
PravinMishra@Pravin-MacBook-Pro ~ git commit -m "added more styling"
[develop 920bcd32ac] added more styling
 1 file changed, 1 insertion(+), 1 deletion(-)
```

Figure 5.8: *Output of command 'git commit -m "added more styling"'*

Now that we have successfully committed our changes on the develop branch without affecting the code from the master branch, let's check whether our code from the master branch is affected or not.

Now, let's see the output of `git log` command, as shown in *Figure* 5.9:

```
PravinMishra@Pravin-MacBook-Pro ~ %git checkout master
Switched to branch 'master'

This repository is configured for Git LFS but 'git-lfs' was not found on your path. If you no longer wish
 the 'post-checkout' file in the hooks directory (set by 'core.hookspath'; usually '.git/hooks').

PravinMishra@Pravin-MacBook-Pro ~ %git log
commit 8d47831ce581706c6842220bcafed15dab732860 (HEAD -> master, origin/master, bugfix2, bugfix1)
Author: pravinmishra2907 <152183287+pravinmishra2907@users.noreply.github.com>
Date:   Tue Nov 28 13:12:14 2023 +0530

    Update index.html

    removed white lines

commit 40d6e3faf26b0e197c587a977eb80f90b7f17eed
Author: Pravin_Mishra <"email>
Date:   Tue Nov 28 13:07:24 2023 +0530

     done
```

Figure 5.9: *Output of command "git log"*

As observed, the master branch does not have the `style.css` file that was added to the develop branch.

Now, if you check our `style.css` file here, you will notice that the changes we made from the develop branch are not present here, indicating that the changes made in the new branch will not affect any file from the master branch. This shows how we can switch to a different branch using `git checkout` and work on the code without affecting the main code from the default master branch.

As discussed earlier, you can also use `git checkout` to revert to a previous commit or version of your code if you need to undo some changes.

Let's understand this with an example.

Suppose you are working on a website project and have made some changes to the code that you are not happy with. You want to go back to a previous version of the code to undo those changes.

To do this, you will first use the `git log` command to find the commit hash, as shown in *Figure* 5.10, which represents the state of the code:

```
PravinMishra@Pravin-MacBook-Pro~ git log
commit 763620847e86665fe7beacf437301fce1dc90a68 (HEAD -> main)
Author: Pravin Mishra <hello@pravinmishra.in>
Date:   Wed Mar 13 10:47:54 2024 +0200

    Fix navigation bar alignment issue on mobile devices

commit fc938ecce3162b14b0ca3d025a24d5ed452062e6
Author: Pravin Mishra <hello@pravinmishra.in>
Date:   Tue Mar 12 05:09:03 2024 +0200

    added style.css

commit 355201f052e824eaeb24a544daaff86023834de9
Author: Pravin Mishra <hello@pravinmishra.in>
Date:   Tue Mar 12 05:02:14 2024 +0200

    modified index.html and added style.css
PravinMishra@Pravin-MacBook-Pro~
```

Figure 5.10: *Output of command "git log"*

To switch to that version of the code, you would use the `git checkout` command with the commit hash: `git checkout 'fc938ecce3162b14b0ca3d025a24d5ed452062e6'`:

```
PravinMishra@Pravin-MacBook-Pro~ git checkout 'fc938ecce3162b14b0ca3d025a24d5ed452062e6'
Previous HEAD position was 7636208 Fix navigation bar alignment issue on mobile devices
HEAD is now at fc938ec added style.css
PravinMishra@Pravin-MacBook-Pro~
```

Figure 5.11: *Output of command "git checkout"*

After pressing Enter, you will be at the `fc938ecce3162b14b0ca3d025a24d5ed452062e6` commit, as shown in *Figure* 5.11. From there, you can see the code as it was at that time and either work on it directly or create a new branch based on that state.

For example, you might create a new branch called `old-version` based on the `'fc938ecce3162b14b0ca3d025a24d5ed452062e6' commit: "git checkout -b old-version"`. This branch will contain the code present at the `fc938ecce3162b14b0ca3d025a24d5ed452062e6`. You can then work on that branch without affecting the original code.

To switch back to the new branch that we need to create and switch to that branch, use the following command:

Command:

```
Git checkout -b old-version
```

Explanation:

Here, you are already familiar with the meaning or use of `git checkout` command.

_b = Command used to create a branch.

Old version = Here, this is the branch name.

Let's see the output of the preceding command in the terminal, as shown in *Figure* 5.12:

```
PravinMishra@Pravin-MacBook-Pro ~ git checkout -b old-version
Switched to a new branch 'old-version'
PravinMishra@Pravin-MacBook-Pro ~ git branch
  Pravin_Cloud
  develop
  i18n-sync-client
  i18n-sync-curriculum
  main
  master
* old-version
  prod-staging
  test_pravin
```

Figure 5.12: *Output of command "git checkout -b old-version"*

Reasons for Creating a New Branch ("old-version")

Let's discuss the reasons for creating a new branch (here, `old-version`). Creating a new branch (`old-version`) serves several purposes, such as:

1. **Isolation**: Changes made in the `old-version` branch are isolated from the main branch, allowing you to work on the reverted code without impacting ongoing development.
2. **Parallel Development**: You can simultaneously work on the `old-version` branch and the main branch, enabling parallel development of different features or bug fixes.
3. **Clear Version History**: Keeping the changes in a separate branch maintains a clear version history. It is easier to understand the context of changes and simplifies the process of merging or discarding the `old-version` branch later.

Later, if you need to switch back to the latest version of the code, you can use `git checkout` again to return to the branch. For example, if you are working on the `master` branch, you can switch back to it with `git checkout master`. This will move your repository back to the most recent commit on the `master` branch, allowing you to continue work on the code from there.

Let's consider a scenario where we switch to the `git checkout master` branch, as shown in *Figure* 5.13:

```
PravinMishra@Pravin-MacBook-Pro ~ git checkout master
Switched to branch 'master'
```

***Figure* 5.13**: *Output of command "git checkout master"*

We have successfully switched to the master branch.

Now, let's open our terminal and enter `git log` to retrieve the hash commit. The output of the preceding command is shown in *Figure* 5.14:

```
PravinMishra@Pravin-MacBook-Pro ~ %git log
commit 8d47831ce581706c6842220bcafed15dab732860 (HEAD -> master, origin/master, bugfix2, bugfix1)
Author: pravinmishra2907 <152183287+pravinmishra2907@users.noreply.github.com>
Date:   Tue Nov 28 13:12:14 2023 +0530

    Update index.html

    removed white lines
```

***Figure* 5.14**: *Output of command "git log"*

To revert to this commit, copy the hash commit and paste it into the command `git checkout <hash commit>`, and then press *Enter*. To check this, refer to *Figure* 5.15:

```
PravinMishra@Pravin-MacBook-Pro ~ %git checkout 8d47831ce581706c6842220bcafed15dab732860
D       pravin.txt
Note: switching to '8d47831ce581706c6842220bcafed15dab732860'.
```

***Figure* 5.15**: *Output of command "git checkout hash commit"*

You can see that the switch to this commit ID (here ID **is 8d47831...**, as shown in *Figure* 5.17) is successful.

Let's navigate to VS code and check our code; you will notice have the previous version of our code available. This demonstrates how we can switch to any previous version of our code.

It's important to note that when we switch to the previous version, at that time you can see that we are not at the master branch, instead we are at the old version branch. So, let's switch back to the master branch.

This demonstrates how the `git checkout` command can be used to switch between different branches and revert to a previous commit or version of your code.

We have created a new develop branch and made modified our code for style.css from that branch. Now that we are satisfied with those modifications and want to apply them to our `style.css` from the master branch, we can use a command called `git merge`.

Basically, git merge is a command used to merge different branches into one branch. We will delve deeper into `git merge` in the next section.

Git Merge

`Git merge` is a command in Git that allows you to combine changes from one branch to another branch.

In Git, you can have different versions of your project saved in different branches. Each branch can have its own changes and updates. When you are ready to combine these changes and updates, you can use `git merge`.

This is particularly useful when you need to add new features or fix bugs in a separate branch before combining those changes with the main branch, that is, the **master branch** of your project.

Let's understand this with the help of an example.

Imagine you and your team are working on building a website together. To keep things organized, you split up the work into different sections and assign each section to a different team member. Each team member works on their own branch in Git.

When everyone is done with their changes, you need to combine all the sections back into one main branch so that the website is complete. This is where `git merge` comes in - it allows you to merge the changes made in each separate branch back into the master branch.

To do this, you would first switch to the master branch of the website using the `git checkout master` command. Then, you would use the `git merge` command followed by the branch name that you want to merge in the master branch. This will merge the changes made in the new branch back into the main branch.

For example, let's say that one team member was responsible for creating the homepage of the website in their own branch, and another team member was responsible for creating the `About Us` page in a separate branch. Once both branches will complete, you can use `git merge` to merge the changes made in both branches back into the main branch.

However, sometimes there can be conflicts between the changes made in different branches, especially if two or more people have made changes to the same section of the website. When this happens, Git will pause the merge process and ask you to manually resolve the conflict before the merge can be completed.

Let's understand this concept by using *Figure* 5.16:

```
        <p>Email: hello@pravinmishra.in</p>
<<<<<<< HEAD
        <p>Phone: 456444</p>
=======
        <p>Phone: 636363</p>
>>>>>>> b122391 (updating phone number)
</body>
```

***Figure* 5.16**: *Showing the conflicts between different branches*

As can be seen in the preceding figure, there is a conflict in the Phone number, where the Remote has phone number `456444` while the local branch has phone number `636363`. In such cases, team members making these respective changes must sync and decide which phone number should be kept. This is how conflicts are resolved, and once resolved, the final results should be committed.

Now, let's explore the concepts of fast-forward merges and normal merges without conflicts in Git.

Fast-Forward Merge

A fast-forward merge occurs when the branch being merged into (typically the main branch) has not diverged from the branch being merged (feature branch). In other words, there are no new commits on the main branch since the feature branch was created. The process is straightforward, and Git can simply "fast-forward" the main branch pointer to the latest commit on the feature branch.

Normal Merge Without Conflicts

A normal merge without conflicts occurs when changes made in two different branches do not overlap or conflict with each other. Git automatically integrates the changes from one branch into another, creating a new commit that represents the merge.

Once the conflict is resolved, Git will merge the changes from different branches together. This is how changes made by different team members can be combined into one branch.

Since we have made some changes to our code from the develop branch, let's merge this with the master branch. Enter the command `git merge develop` in the Terminal and press Enter, as shown in *Figure 5.17*:

```
PravinMishra@Pravin-MacBook-Pro ~ %git merge develop
Updating 8d47831..18d44be
Fast-forward
 index.html | 4 ++--
 1 file changed, 2 insertions(+), 2 deletions(-)
```

Figure 5.17*: Output of command "git merge develop"*

Here, you can see that branches are merged successfully. Now, you will see the changes that we made in the develop branch are now available in the master branch as well. This is how we can merge two branches.

Now let's go in little deeper and understand how to resolve merge conflicts.

Resolving Merge Conflicts

As mentioned earlier, you will encounter merge conflicts frequently. It's very important to understand the best way to resolve this conflict. While merge conflicts might seem troublesome, they aren't scary creatures hiding in your code, waiting to make your life difficult. Essentially, they are simply disagreements between two sets of code. Let's break down the process and take a closer look.

Merge conflicts happen when two branches make changes to the same part of a file and then attempt to merge into one another. Git, although powerful, isn't smart. It won't know which version of the code is correct or the one you prefer. Therefore, it highlights these differences and asks for human intervention to resolve them.

When Git identifies a conflict, it will add markers to your code. These markers include **<<<<<<<**, **=======**, and **>>>>>>>**. These lines surround the conflicting code from both branches. The part before the **=======** is your current branch's code, while the part after it is the conflicting code from the branch you are trying to merge.

Let's see the output in *Figure* 5.18:

```
<<<<<<< HEAD
This change are made from dev branch
=======
This changes is made from dev branch
>>>>>>> 6be5b17 ( testing conflict)
```

Figure 5.18: *Output of the conflicting code*

Steps to Resolve Merge Conflict:

1. **`git status`**: Run `git status` command. It will display the name of the file that has conflicts. The file has been updated on both a remote branch and a local branch, so it will be denoted as both modified in the git status output, as shown in *Figure* 5.19:

```
PravinMishra@Pravin-MacBook-Pro ~ %git status
interactive rebase in progress; onto 29d0ce6
Last command done (1 command done):
   pick b122391 updating phone number
No commands remaining.
You are currently rebasing branch 'master' on '29d0ce6'.
  (fix conflicts and then run "git rebase --continue")
  (use "git rebase --skip" to skip this patch)
  (use "git rebase --abort" to check out the original branch)

Unmerged paths:
  (use "git restore --staged <file>..." to unstage)
  (use "git add <file>..." to mark resolution)
        both modified:   index.html

no changes added to commit (use "git add" and/or "git commit -a")
```

Figure 5.19: *Git status command showing the conflict message*

2. **`Vim index.html`**: The second step is to open the file in any file editor. In this case, we have opened the file using Vim editor, as shown in *Figure* 5.20:

```
PravinMishra@Pravin-MacBook-Pro ~ %vim index.html
```

Figure 5.20: *Output of "index.html"*

3. **Go to the conflicted area**: The conflicted area is present between **<<<<** and **>>>>** annotators. In this example, the phone number is the conflicted part, as shown in *Figure* 5.21:

```
        <p>Email: hello@pravinmishra.in</p>
<<<<<<< HEAD
        <p>Phone: 456444</p>
=======
        <p>Phone: 636363</p>
>>>>>>> b122391 (updating phone number)
</body>
```

Figure 5.21: *Showing the conflict message*

4. **Update the conflicted area**: Keep the desired phone number in the file (in this case, 636363 in the phone number we want to keep in file). Remove the **<<<<** and **>>>>** annotators, and save the updated file, as shown in *Figure* 5.22:

```
            <h2>Contact us</h2>
            <p>Email: hello@pravinmishra.in</p>
            <p>Phone: 636363</p>
</body>
```

***Figure* 5.22**: *Showing the conflict lines are removed*

5. **Push the updated file:** Run the command git add index.html to stage the file and git commit to save the changes to Git and finally git push origin master to push these changes to the remote Git repository. This is how we resolve merge conflicts, as shown in *Figure* 5.23:

```
PravinMishra@Pravin-MacBook-Pro ~ %git add index.html
PravinMishra@Pravin-MacBook-Pro ~ %git commit -m "Resolved merge conflicts"
[detached HEAD f908206] Resolved merge conflicts
 1 file changed, 1 insertion(+), 1 deletion(-)
PravinMishra@Pravin-MacBook-Pro ~ %git push origin master
```

***Figure* 5.23**: *Output of file added and commit message*

Resolving conflicts is an important step in the reverse merging process. It's also important to understand how to stop or cancel the merge if you encounter unexpected issues. Let's understand these aspects in the next section.

Reverse Merging with Conflict Resolution

Reverse merging is a process in Git where you merge changes from a forward commit or set of commits into a previous state of your project, effectively "undoing" some changes. It is not a standard term in Git, but it generally refers to a situation where you want to reverse the effects of one or more commits. This is typically done using the git revert command.

When conflicts arise during this process, they must be resolved manually just like any other merge conflict in Git. Here's how you can perform a reverse merge and resolve conflicts:

Step 1: Identify the Commit to Reverse

First, you need to identify the commit or commits that you want to reverse. You can use `git log` to review the commit history and find the commit hashes of the changes you want to undo.

Step 2: Reverse the Commit

Once you have identified the commit, use `git revert` followed by the commit hash.

If you are reverting more than one commit, you can either run git revert for each commit individually or use a range of commits:

```
git revert <commit-hash>
# or for a range of commits
git revert <newer-commit-hash>^..<older-commit-hash>
```

This command will create a new commit that undoes the changes introduced by the specified commit(s).

Step 3: Resolve Any Conflicts

If the revert process results in conflicts, Git will pause and allow you to fix them before completing the revert.

Edit the files listed with conflicts and adjust the code to resolve the discrepancies.

Look for the conflict markers <<<<<<<, =======, and >>>>>>> in your files. The code between <<<<<<< HEAD and ======= is your current code, and the code between ======= and >>>>>>> <commit-hash> is the code from the commit you are trying to revert.

After resolving each conflict in a file, use `git add <file>` to mark it as resolved.

Step 4: Finalize the Revert

Once all conflicts are resolved, you can finalize the revert by continuing the operation:

```
git revert --continue
```

Git will then complete the revert operation and create a new commit that reflects the reversal of the specified commit(s).

Step 5: Test the Changes

After the revert and conflict resolution are complete, thoroughly test your code to ensure that it works as expected and that no additional issues have been introduced.

Step 6: Push the Changes

Finally, once you are satisfied with the changes and have tested them, push the new commit to your remote repository:

```
git push origin <branch-name>
```

This will update the remote repository with the reverse merge changes.

So, as you have seen, reverse merging with conflict resolution is a powerful feature of Git that allows you to maintain control over your project's history and make necessary adjustments. As with any complex operation, it should be performed carefully.

It's advisable to do this in a separate branch to avoid disrupting the main line of development until you are certain the reverse merge is successful.

Stopping or Cancelling the Merge

To stop or cancel the merge process, you can use the following command:

Stop the Merge Process:

```
git merge -abort
```

If you encounter unexpected issues or conflicts that you are unable to resolve, you might want to stop the merge process. This command cancels the merge, returning your branch to the state it was in before the merge attempt.

Review Changes and Retry:

After stopping the merge, review the conflicting changes, address any issues, and retry the merge process. Repeat the conflict resolution and commit steps until the merge is successful.

For Example

Imagine reading two versions of the same story. Both stories are nearly identical, but in one version, the main character's name is '*Ram*,' and in the other, it's '*Shyam*.' You have to decide which name to keep or maybe even come up with a new one.

Once you have made your decision (which means you have selected either the Ram or Shyam character for understanding, as used in the preceding paragraph) and edited the code to your satisfaction, you need to remove those markers. This signals to Git that the conflict is resolved. Then, follow the usual process: use `git add` to stage the changes, followed by `git commit` to confirm the merge.

While understanding how to resolve merge conflicts, fostering good communication within your team is equally important. It has been noticed that many merge conflicts arise due to a lack of communication. For example, if two team members are unaware that they are editing the same piece of code, it's likely to result in a merge conflict.

So, besides becoming familiar with the resolution process, always make it a habit to sync up with your team regularly, especially if you are all working remotely. Use collaboration tools, have daily stand-ups, or simply chat informally about what everyone's working on. This not only reduces merge conflicts but also streamlines the development process, ensuring everyone works together smoothly.

As we continue our exploration of Git, always remember that tools are here to help, not hinder. Merge conflicts, although sometimes a bit tedious, are a crucial part of version control. They ensure every piece of code is reviewed, and nothing gets overlooked. With time and practice, you will find that they are not roadblocks but rather checkpoints ensuring everything is on track.

Best Practices and Common Pitfalls

Here are some best practices and common pitfalls to consider when working in the world of version control.

Commit Often

Imagine a scenario where you are building a puzzle. If you were to lose a piece, it would be easier to figure out where it fits if you only had a handful of pieces scattered around, rather than hundreds. Similarly, when you commit your changes frequently in smaller chunks, it becomes easier to track and manage your work. If something goes wrong, you know exactly where to look because the affected codebase is smaller. Moreover, frequent commits help in documenting the progress. Every commit serves as a checkpoint. If you find that a particular approach isn't working, you can easily revert to one of the previous checkpoints without losing much work.

Contrast this with infrequent, large commits. If an error sneaks in, it becomes an uphill task to find and fix. Large commits obscure the history, making it tough to understand when and why a certain change was introduced.

Avoid Long-Lived Branches

When you create a branch and keep it separate for too long without merging it back to the main branch, you are essentially creating a parallel universe of your code. With time, the main branch progresses, new features are added, bugs are fixed, and so on. Now, when you finally decide to merge your long-lived branch, you face a multitude of conflicts because the two branches have diverged considerably. Resolving these conflicts becomes a mammoth task, consuming precious developer hours.

When dealing with long-lived branches that have diverged considerably from the main branch, it's essential to keep them updated to minimize conflicts during eventual merging. One effective strategy for maintaining such branches is reverse merging, also known as **merge from main** or **upmerge**

It feels like you are solving a jigsaw puzzle where half the pieces don't fit. Merging becomes a game of guesswork, where you are not sure which parts of the code to keep and which to discard.

Consistent Commit Messages

Each entry (commit) tells a story of what was done and why. A well-structured commit message serves two primary purposes. First, for you (or any other developer) to look back and understand the reasoning behind a particular change. Second, in collaborative projects, to inform team members about the changes made.

Imagine having to figure out the purpose of a commit labelled **fixes** or **updates.** You would have to dive into the code to understand what "*fixes*" or "*updates*" refer to. A more descriptive message, such as "*Fixed login bug caused by an uninitialized variable*" gives a clear picture instantly.

So, what makes for a good format?

Based on experience in the field, an effective structure consists of a short, descriptive title followed by a more detailed explanation (if needed).

Real-World Scenarios and Solutions

Throughout a long career in IT, numerous issues arise, especially related to branching and merging. Sharing some of these scenarios can offer insights to budding developers.

Scenario 1

Once, in a project, two team members were working on separate branches. Both had to modify the same function but for different reasons. They made their changes and tested their respective branches – everything worked fine. However, when it was time to merge both branches into the main one, chaos ensued. The function failed because both modifications were incompatible.

Solution

The immediate solution was to hold a meeting between the two developers. They reviewed the function, discussed their changes, and came up with a unified solution that catered to both requirements. This incident highlighted the importance of regular communication in a team, especially when working on related features.

Scenario 2

In another project, we were nearing a release. One developer, eager to fix as many bugs as possible, decided to stay late and push a series of commits. The next day, the main branch was riddled with new, unforeseen bugs.

Solution

We realized the developer hadn't tested the changes sufficiently. To solve this, we decided to enforce a rule: **no direct commits to the main branch**, especially close to a release. Instead, all changes were to be made on separate branches, reviewed by peers, and then merged.

Such incidents are common in the IT world. The key takeaway is to learn from mistakes and always strive to streamline workflows, ensuring smooth operations.

Conclusion

As we conclude the chapter on branching and merging, we have explored the fundamental aspects of handling and moving through different lines of development in Git. We have understood the importance of branches in our projects and have become skilled at making and moving around these branches using commands like `git branch` and `git checkout`. This knowledge is essential for effectively managing different versions of your code. Additionally, we have looked at combining different pieces of work through `git merge` and have dealt with the sometimes-difficult job of fixing merge conflicts.

This chapter aims to equip you with best practices and strategies to avoid common pitfalls that might occur during branching and merging. Through real-world scenarios and solutions, we have seen how these practices are applied in everyday coding situations, ensuring that you are not just following commands but also understanding their applications and implications.

In the next chapter, we will learn about GitHub - how we can push our code to the GitHub repository from our local Git repository and how we can pull code from the GitHub repository to our local Git repository. However, as always, it's vital to ensure a strong foundation. Practice branching and merging until you are comfortable with the process. Remember, every challenge you face is an opportunity to learn and grow.

CHAPTER 6
Introduction to GitHub

Introduction

In this chapter, we will discuss GitHub, the world's most popular platform for software developers to come together and collaborate. If you are not already familiar with it, by the end of this chapter, you will see why it has been the preferred choice for many professionals for over a decade.

Structure

In this chapter, we will cover the following topics:

- Understanding the Essence and Value of GitHub
- Familiarization with Pivotal Terminologies Associated with GitHub
- Setting Up Your GitHub Account for Optimum Efficiency
- Vital Tips for Newcomers to the Platform
- Initiating Your Very First Repository on GitHub

By the end of this chapter, you will not only understand what GitHub is and why it is important for developers but also have the confidence to create and manage your first repository on this platform.

Understanding GitHub

GitHub is a Remote Repository Management Platform on which users can manage their code and collaborate with other users. It helps users to work on the same code remotely, without messing it up or creating conflicts. In the way that Google Docs is used to collaborate on a document with others, GitHub similarly allows developers to collaborate on coding projects.

GitHub is a platform that uses a version control system called Git to help developers manage and collaborate on software projects.

With the help of Git, you can create a local repository and manage the source code in that local repository available within your work system. GitHub, however, allows you to create repositories in a remote location that is accessible over the internet. Code will be developed in your work system and tracked using Git, and once the code is ready, it will be merged in the remote branch available in the remote repository created on GitHub, using the `git push` command.

Other developers can also push their code in the same remote repository, and you can get that code merged from the remote branch to your local branch using the `git pull` command.

Thus, with GitHub, you can store your code in a central location that is accessible to everyone in your team, or publicly, depending on the type of repository you create. We will discuss the types of repositories in the upcoming sections. On GitHub, you can make changes to the code, track those changes over time, and collaborate with others to build better code. GitHub is also a great place to learn from other developers and contribute to open-source projects.

History and Importance of GitHub

Back in 2008, the world of software development witnessed the birth of a platform that would redefine collaboration and code management. This platform was GitHub.

When GitHub was first introduced, the idea of a platform that could host version-controlled code repositories on the cloud was relatively new. What truly set GitHub apart was not just its functionality, but also its vision. From its inception, GitHub aimed not only to provide a service but also to create a global community of developers. This vision resonated with many, and resulted in its rapid adoption by developers, both newbies and seasoned, from all corners of the world.

Upon reflection over the years after its launch, a few notable observations stand out. First, the sheer volume of code hosted on GitHub is tremendous. With the availability of millions of repositories, GitHub has become the biggest remote repository manager in the world. However, the number of projects is just one side of the story. The real magic lies in the diversity of these projects, ranging from simple personal scripts to complex software used by millions.

What is also truly heartening is the community that has blossomed around GitHub, a community in which knowledge is freely shared, help is always at hand, and collaboration is the norm. It reminds me of the early days of my career when sharing was done through forums and emails. GitHub took that spirit, and amplified it, providing tools that made collaboration intuitive and efficient.

Now, let us discuss an open source. The beauty of open source lies in its transparency, and is rooted in the idea that software, as a product of human intellect, should be accessible to all. GitHub became the perfect home for such projects. The platform not only made it easy for developers to share their code but also provided tools to encourage collaboration, be it through pull requests or issues.

The commitment of GitHub to open source is evident in its features, such as the ability for anyone to `fork` a project, make improvements, and then propose those changes back to the original project via a `pull request` changed software development. This means that you do not need to be part of a company or a select group to contribute to a project, all you need is expertise, and the will.

It is not an exaggeration to say that the biggest tech giants today owe a part of their success to open sources and, by extension, to GitHub. Be it tools, libraries, or entire frameworks, many of the technologies that these companies use or build upon are hosted on GitHub.

The following are some simple examples of widely used technologies that users can easily relate to, all of which are hosted on GitHub:

jQuery

- **Type**: JavaScript Library
- **GitHub Repository**: jQuery
- **Description**: jQuery simplifies common JavaScript tasks, making it easier for developers to manipulate HTML documents and handle events.

VS Code

- **Type**: Code Editor
- **GitHub Repository**: Visual Studio Code
- **Description**: Visual Studio Code is a popular and user-friendly code editor developed by Microsoft, known for its versatility and extensive features

Bootstrap

- **Type**: Front-end Framework
- **GitHub Repository**: Bootstrap
- **Description**: Bootstrap is a widely used framework that helps developers create responsive and visually appealing websites with pre-designed components

However, it is not just the giants, but individual developers who also benefit immensely from GitHub. Over the years, I have hosted my projects, contributed to others, learned from the vast pool of shared knowledge, and even found collaboration opportunities on GitHub.

Thus, when we talk about the history and importance of GitHub, we are not just discussing a platform, but a revolution in how we think about code, collaboration, and community. GitHub has been a pivotal part of the journey in IT and holds the same place of importance for countless others.

Open-Source Projects

Open-source projects are like group projects that anyone can join and work on together. It is a fantastic way to learn from others, share your ideas, and positively impact the coding community.

An open-source project is a software project in which the source code is made available for others to view, use, and modify.

For example, let us say a developer creates an open-source project on GitHub for a simple calculator application. The source code for the calculator would be available on GitHub, allowing other developers to download the code, modify it, and contribute to the project. Another developer might add a new feature to the calculator, such as a button for calculating square roots. Another developer might fix a bug in the code that was causing errors. The original developer could review the changes, merge them into the main codebase, and release a new version of the calculator with the new features and bug fixes.

When a software project is made open source on GitHub, other developers can contribute to it by improving or adding new features. This makes the project better over time, which benefits both developers and users. Additionally, other developers can learn from the code and use it to create their projects.

Now, let us understand exactly how GitHub works.

Understanding the Workings of GitHub

Let us see the definition of GitHub: **GitHub** is a web-based platform for version control and collaborative software development. It facilitates the hosting of software projects, provides version control using Git, and offers a range of features for collaboration, code review, and project management.

Features of GitHub

GitHub has many features. Some of the important features of GitHub are as follows:

- **Code Storage**: GitHub is a platform that helps people store and organize their computer code. It is like a virtual locker in which you can keep your code files safe and accessible from any device that is connected to the internet.

- **Version Control**: One of the main benefits of GitHub is that it has a version control system that tracks changes made to your code over time. This means that you can see who made what changes, and you can easily go back to earlier versions of your code if needed.
- **Collaboration Tool**: GitHub is also great for collaborating with others on your code projects. You can invite other people to work on your code, keep track of issues and bugs, and merge changes made by other people into your codebase. You can choose whether to make your repositories public or private, depending on whether you want to share your code with others or keep it private.

Community Resources: GitHub has a large and active community of developers who contribute to open-source projects and share code snippets and resources. This can be a valuable source of knowledge and inspiration for learning and improving your coding skills.

These are some of the most important features of GitHub.

These features collectively make GitHub a comprehensive platform for version control, collaboration, and project management, supporting developers and teams throughout the software development lifecycle.

GitHub allows us to create a remote repository, that is a repository hosted on the internet, and we can store our code in that repository so we can track changes made to our code. It also allows us to work in collaboration with other developers.

Using Git, we can store the code in a local repository on our local system, whereas using GitHub, we can store the code in a remote repository that is hosted on the internet so that we can access the code from anywhere.

Imagine, for example, a group of friends working on a project to create a website, but they are at different locations. Each friend has a copy of the code on their computer. They can make changes to the code and upload it to the GitHub repository so that everyone can see the changes.

GitHub also helps to keep track of any problems or new ideas that come up during the project. If someone finds a problem, they can report it on GitHub, and the team can work together to fix it.

Let us say you are using an open-source project on GitHub that is a calculator application. While using the application, you encounter an issue that the output for some multiplication shows the wrong result. In this case, you may want to report the issue to the manager of the project, so that they can investigate and fix the problem.

When we create a remote repository using GitHub, we can make the repository private or public.

Let us first understand the concept of a public repository.

Public Repository

A public repository is like an open book that anyone can read. It is like sharing your project with the whole world. This means that the code in a public repository can be seen by anyone on the internet.

Let us understand this with a simple example.

Let us say you are a chef who wants to share your favorite recipe with the world. You decide to create a public recipe book in GitHub on which anyone can access your recipe.

By making your recipe book public, anyone can view and use your recipe. Other chefs can also contribute their recipes, or suggest changes to your recipe. This allows for collaboration and sharing among the cooking community.

A public repository is a great option if you want to share your project with others, get feedback, and collaborate with a larger community of developers.

Thus, we can create a private or public remote repository on GitHub, and store our code files in it. This is one of the features of GitHub.

Private Repository

A **private repository** is a locked folder that only you and the people you invite can access. It is like having a secret club to which only members are allowed. This means that the code in a private repository can only be seen and worked on by you and the people you permit. It is a great option if you want to work on a project without making your code accessible to the public.

Let us say you are a software developer working on a proprietary project for a company. The project contains sensitive information that cannot be shared with the public, and you need a secure place to store and collaborate on the code. In this case, you could create a private repository on GitHub for the project.

By making the repository private, only you and authorized collaborators, such as other developers or team members, have access to the code. This provides an added layer of security and privacy for the project, ensuring that the code and any sensitive information it contains are not shared with unauthorized individuals.

Setting Up Your GitHub Account for Success

In the previous section, we studied what GitHub is, how it works, and learned about its important features.

In this section, let us understand how to create a GitHub account.

To work on GitHub, and to create a remote repository and store your code file in that repository, you have to create a GitHub account.

Let us see how you can create a GitHub repository.

Steps to Create a GitHub Repository

To create an account on GitHub, first go to https://github.com, and click on the **Sign up** button in the top-right corner of the page:

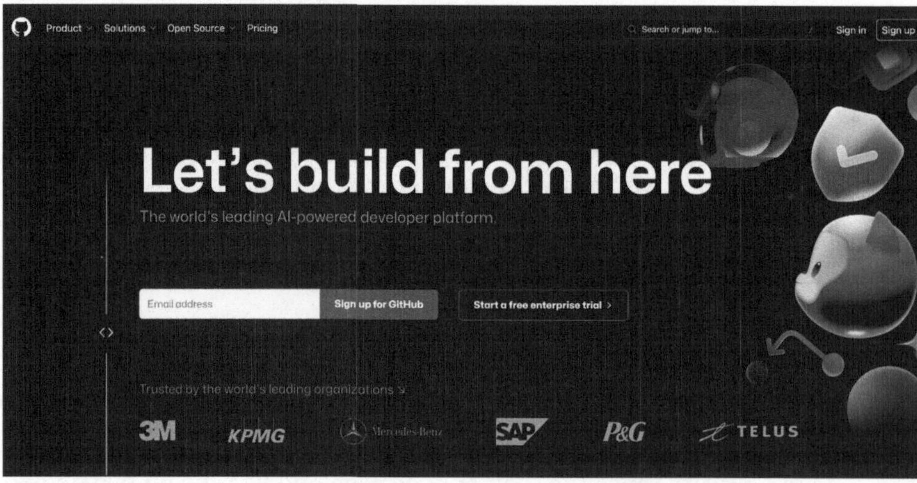

Figure 6.1: *Image of the "Sign-Up" page*

Now, you will need to fill out the sign-up form with your information. Start by choosing a username that you will use to log in to your account. It is important to choose a username that is easy to remember

Next, enter your email address, and create a strong, unique password. You can also choose to sign up with your Google account or your Apple ID if you prefer.

Once you have filled out the form, click the green **Create account** button.

Congratulations! You have successfully created a GitHub account. You can now start using GitHub to store and share your code projects, collaborate with others, and learn from the community.

After you have created your account, you will be taken to your GitHub dashboard, on which you can create GitHub remote repositories, join organizations, and explore the GitHub community.

Now, let us understand GitHub organization.

GitHub Organization

A GitHub organization is like a virtual workspace in which a group of people can collaborate on software projects. It helps them organize their code, work together more effectively, and manage who can access the projects. Think of it like a shared digital office for a team working on a project together.

When you create an organization on GitHub, you can invite other people to join as members or collaborators. Members have full access to everything in the organization, such as creating new projects and managing who else can join. Collaborators have more limited access, and can only work on specific projects or parts of the code.

The **Explore** option on the GitHub dashboard allows you to discover interesting repositories and users on the platform. It is like a search engine for GitHub that suggests repositories and users based on different criteria.

Let us click the **Explore** option, and you will see several sections that showcase different repositories and users:

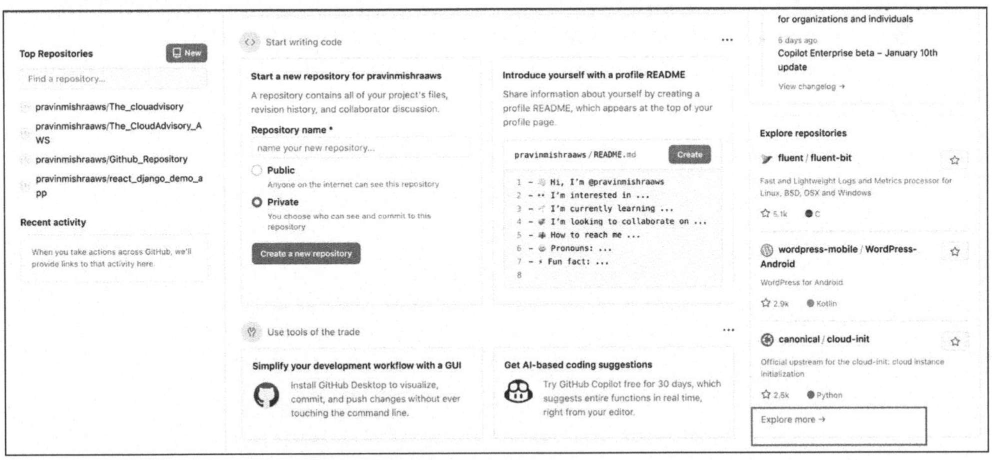

***Figure 6.2**: Showing the explore option*

After clicking the **Explore more** option, we will go to the home page that shows several options, as shown in *Figure 6.3*:

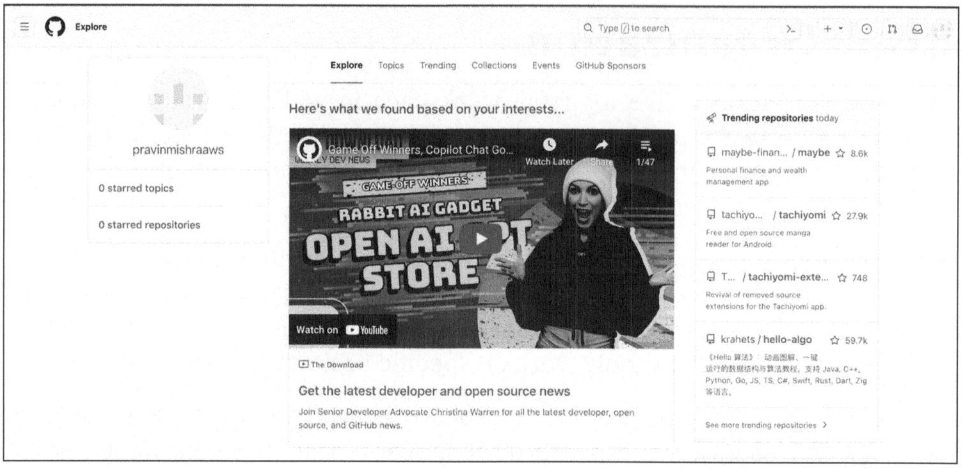

Figure 6.3: *Homepage of the GitHub account showing several options*

Let us discuss these options one by one, as follows:

1. **`Trending`**: This section shows the repositories that are currently popular on GitHub, based on the number of stars, forks, and other metrics. This can be a great way to discover new and interesting projects. *Figure* 6.4 shows the Trending option:

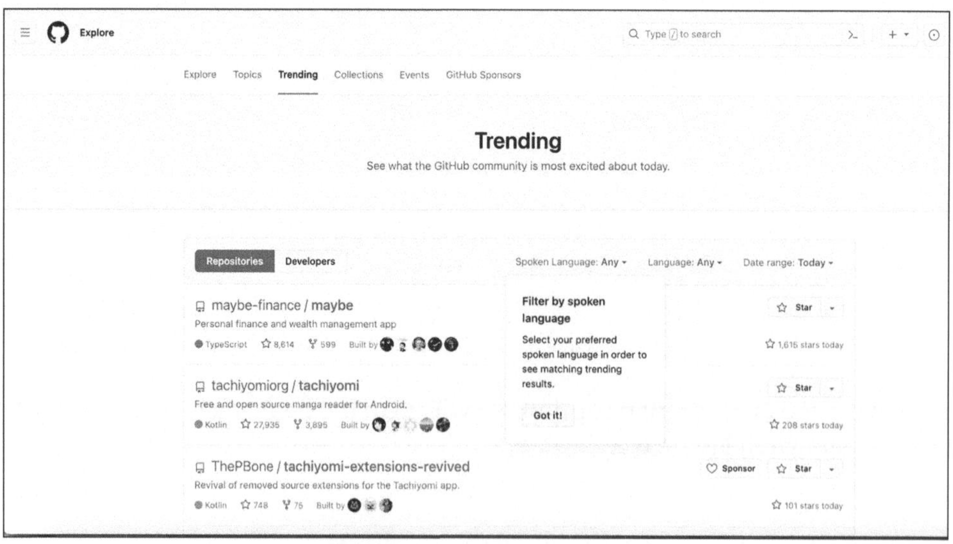

Figure 6.4: *Trending option*

2. **`Topics`**: This section shows repositories that are categorized by different topics, such as machine learning, web development, or game development. You can click on a topic to see a list of related repositories.

Figure 6.5 shows the **`Topics`** option:

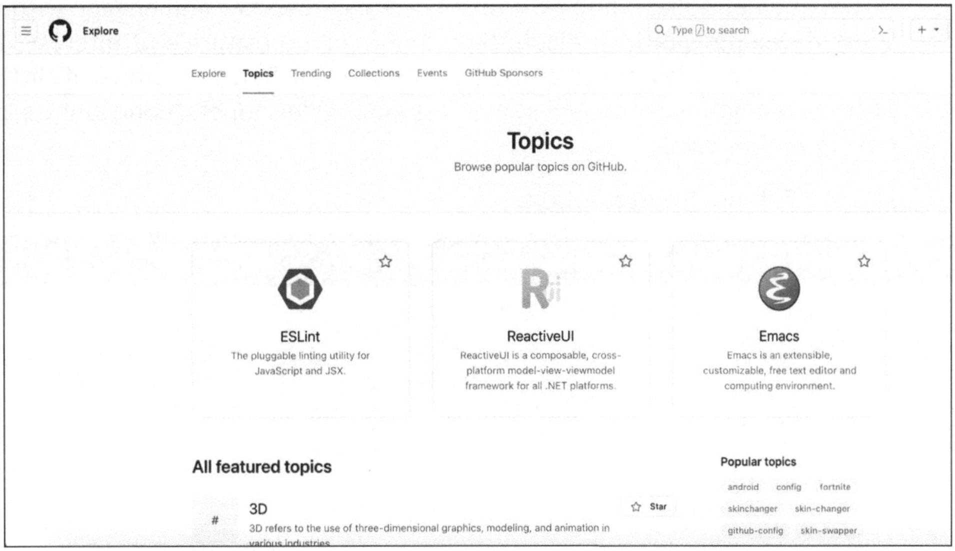

***Figure 6.5**: "Topics" option*

3. **`Collections`**: This section shows collections of repositories that have been curated by GitHub users or organizations. These collections can be based on different themes or topics, such as open-source projects, front-end development, or data science.

   Figure 6.6 shows the **`Collections`** option:

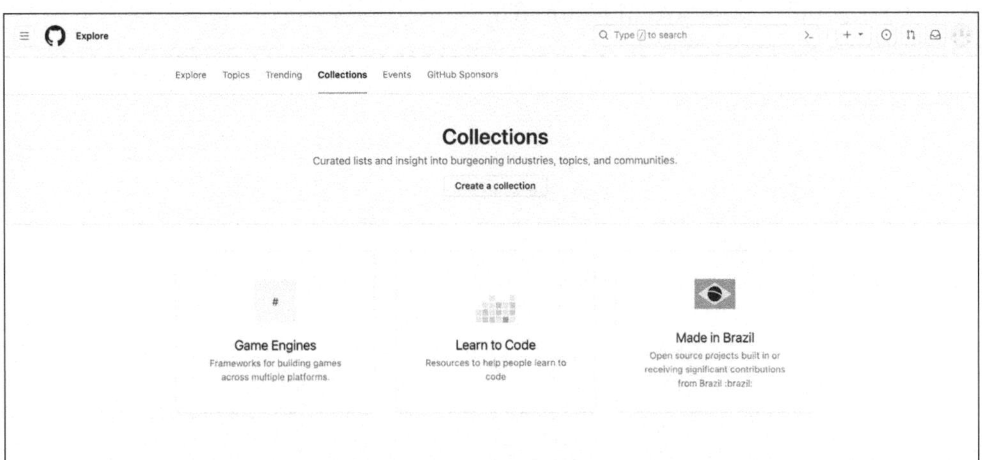

***Figure 6.6**: "Collections" option*

4. **`Events`**: In the **`Events`** section of GitHub's Explore option, users can stay informed about activities and updates across repositories and organizations. Events showcase a dynamic feed of recent actions, including opened issues,

pull requests, code pushes, and discussions within the GitHub community. It serves as a centralized hub on which users can discover and engage with the latest developments in projects they follow or repositories of interest. The Events feed provides valuable insights into the collaborative nature of GitHub, fostering communication and awareness among developers, contributors, and project enthusiasts.

Figure 6.7 shows **`Events`** option:

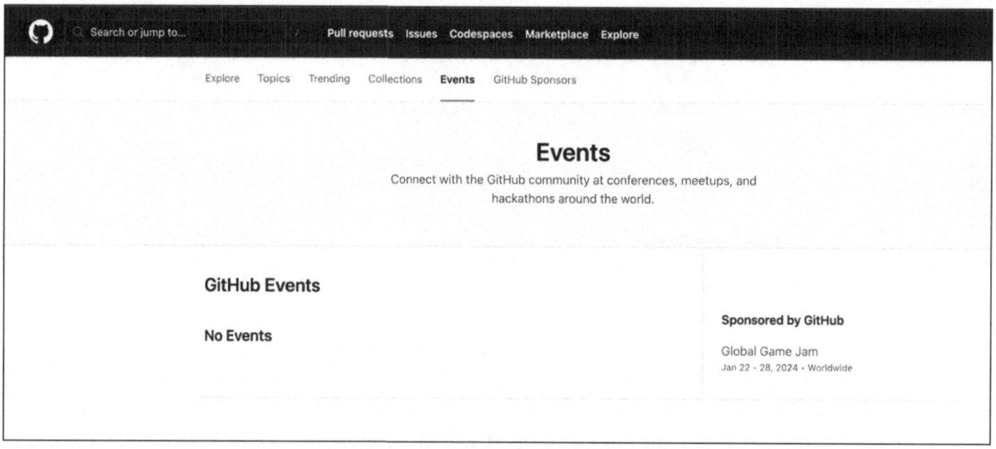

***Figure 6.7**: "Events" option*

5. **`Profile`**: In this section, you will update your information and configuration. To check out your profile, click on the dropdown from the right corner, and select your profile, as shown in *Figure* 6.8:

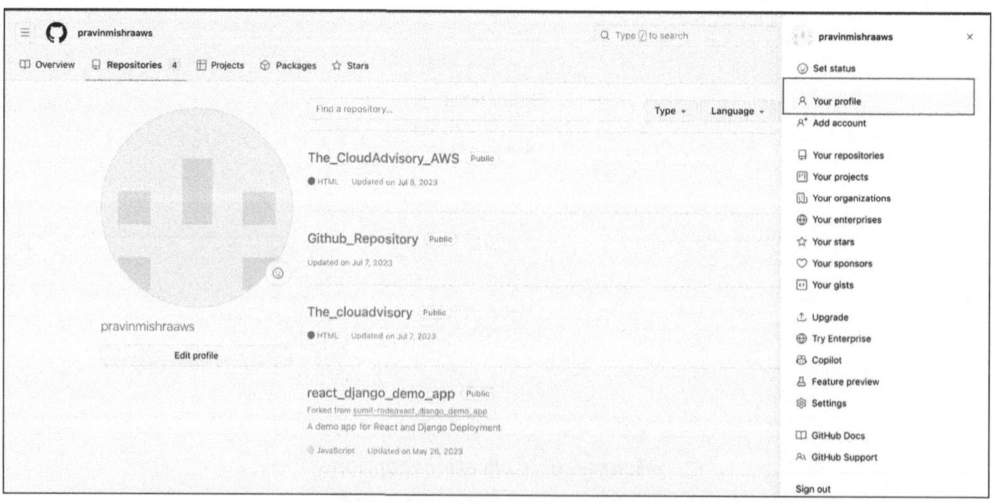

***Figure 6.8**: "Our profile" option*

If you have not created any repositories, then it will show you the message, "*You don't have any public repositories yet*".

In our case, we have created four public repositories, as shown in *Figure* 6.9:

Figure 6.9: *GitHub account of PravinMishra has four public repositories*

And that is it! You now know how to create a GitHub account.

In the next section, we will learn how to create a GitHub repository, and how to link remote and local repositories using the `git remote add` command.

Creating Your First GitHub Repository

As you know, by using GitHub, you can create a remote repository that can be accessed over the internet and used to store the code file in that repository. You also make changes to the code, track those changes over time, and collaborate with others to build better code.

While working with Git, we created a local Git repository for working on our project, and saved our code file in that local repository. Now, suppose we want to save the same code file on the remote repository, then we can do that with GitHub.

To do so, first, **create a remote GitHub repository**.

To create a GitHub repository, first sign into your GitHub account.

Now, click on the dropdown beside the plus (+) icon from the top right corner, and select **`New Repositories`**.

This will redirect you to the page on which you can create a GitHub repository.

Now, to create a GitHub repository, enter the repository name, for example, `The_cloudadvisory`.

If you want, you can also give a repository description, though this is optional.

You will also have the option to select a public repository or a private repository.

For this demonstration, we will select the public mode, as shown in *Figure* 6.10:

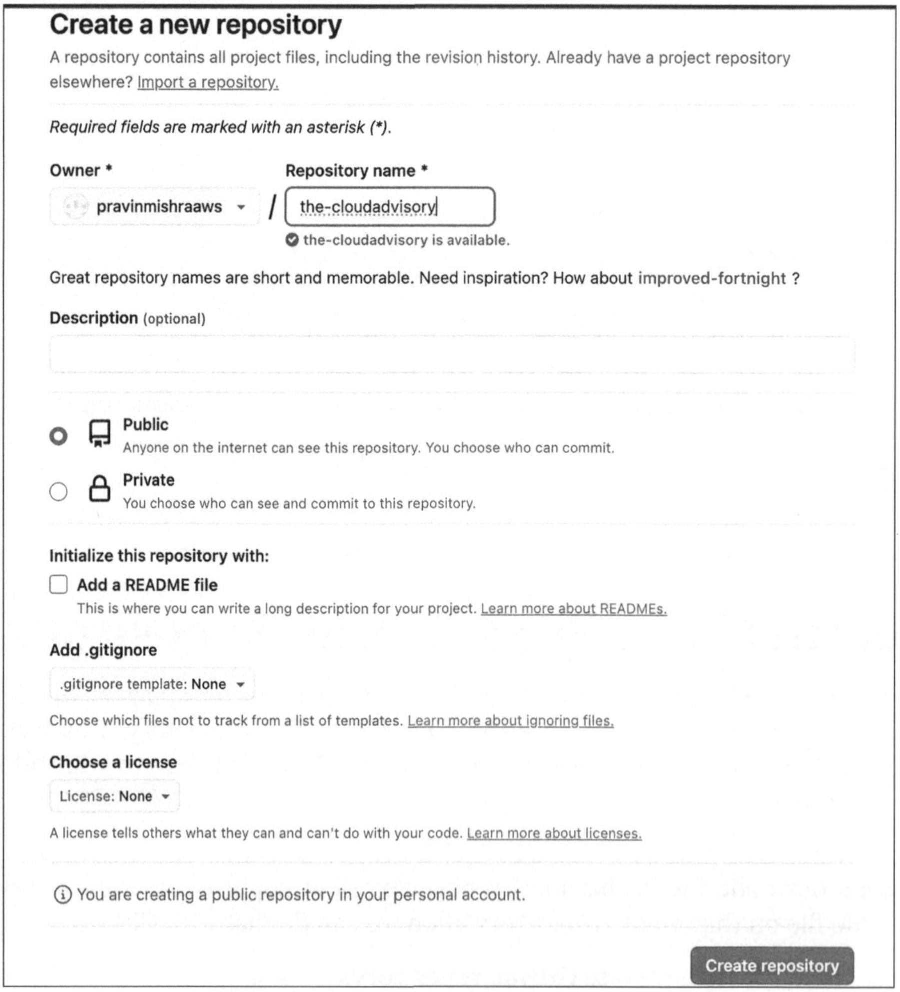

Figure 6.10: *Image of selecting "Public Repository"*

Next, click on **`Create repository`**, and your repository is created.

Important Note: In *Figure* 6.10, we have created `the-clouadvisory` repository, but in *Figure* 6.9, we have shown the list of public repositories. In *Figure* 6.9, one of the public repositories is named `the-clouadvisory`, and in *Figure* 6.10, we show the creation of a new repository, `the-clouadvisory`. While you might get confused with these repositories, note that both the figures showing the same repository, that is `the-clouadvisory`.

On Git, we have to write a command `git init` to initialize a Git repository, but GitHub requires different processes to create a repository, as shown in *Figure* 6.11:

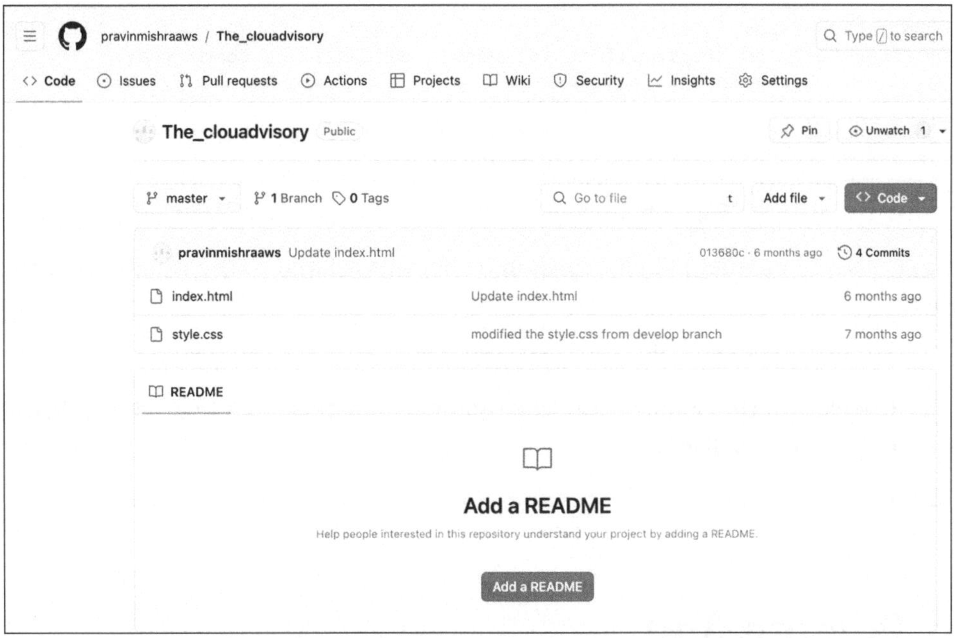

***Figure 6.11**: The "the-clouadvisory" repository created*

Since there are two files in our repository, we are shown some suggestions.

We have created an empty repository on GitHub, and now, to publish or code in the newly created remote repository, we will have to go to Git Bash in our system, and switch to the directory where we have initialized the local repository using the `cd path-to-the-local-repository`:

```
PravinMishra@Pravin-MacBook-Pro ~ % mkdir the_clouadvisory
PravinMishra@Pravin-MacBook-Pro ~ %cd the_clouadvisory
```

***Figure 6.12**: Output of the command "mkdir"*

Run the `git status` command to ensure you are in the Git repository, and verify the output:

```
PravinMishra@Pravin-MacBook-Pro ~ %git status
On branch feature-branch
Changes not staged for commit:
  (use "git add/rm <file>..." to update what will be committed)
  (use "git restore <file>..." to discard changes in working directory)
        deleted:    ../pravin.txt

Untracked files:
  (use "git add <file>..." to include in what will be committed)
        ../pravin_updated.txt

no changes added to commit (use "git add" and/or "git commit -a")
PravinMishra@Pravin-MacBook-Pro ~ %
```

***Figure 6.13**: Output of the command "git status"*

The `git remote` command helps in running actions related to the remote repository, such as :

1. Adding the link for the remote repository to the local Git repository.
2. Checking if the details about the remote repositories are currently linked with our local repository.
3. Updating or deleting the remote repository URL from the local repository

Now, let us understand the `git remote add` in detail.

Git Remote Add

In Git, `git remote add` is a command used to add a URL to the remote repository for the local Git repository. These URLs are used by push, pull, or fetch commands to share or get the latest changes from the remote repository.

Let us understand this through an example.

Let us say you are working on a website project with a team of developers, and you are using Git to manage the code changes. Each developer on your team has a local copy of the website code on their computer, and you need a way to sync all of the changes together.

For example, let us say you create a new repository on GitHub for your website project. You would then copy the URL of the repository (for example, https://github.com/username/repo-name.git).

In our case, we have created the `the_clouadvisory` repository.

Next, on your local computer, you navigate to the directory where you initialized your local repository, and where your website code is stored, and then enter the command `git remote add origin <URL of remote repository>`. This links your remote repository to the local repository with the name "`origin`".

Now let us link our remote repository with our local repository.

First, go to the GitHub remote repository, and copy the repository URL.

Now, go to the terminal. You will notice that we are already at our local Git repository.

Now, enter the command `git remote add origin`, followed by the remote repository URL:

`git remote add origin https://github.com/thecloudadvisory2020/The_cloudadvisory.git`

There is no error, which means both the remote and local repositories are linked successfully.

However, one must verify that there is no error in connecting both the remote and local repositories. For this, use the command `git remote -v`, as shown in *Figure 6.14*:

```
PravinMishra@Pravin-MacBook-Pro ~ %git remote -v
origin  git@github.com:pravinmishra2907/the_cloudadvisory.git (fetch)
origin  git@github.com:pravinmishra2907/the_cloudadvisory.git (push)
PravinMishra@Pravin-MacBook-Pro ~ %
```

***Figure 6.14**: Output of the command "git remote -v"*

Now, you can upload code files from the local repository to the remote repository using the command `git push`, and if there is any file available on your remote repository, then you can download that file to the local repository using the command `git pull`.

Let us learn how to work with Git and GitHub together.

Working with Git and GitHub

In the previous section, we learned about how to create a remote repository, and to link a remote repository with the local repository.

Now, we are going to learn about `git push` and `git pull`.

While we have successfully linked our remote repository and local repository, there are code files in our local repository that are not available in our remote repository even after the link-up is successful. To get those files onto our remote repository, we need to use command, `git push`.

Let us learn about this command.

Git Push

In Git, `git push` is a command that is used to upload the changes you made in your local Git repository to a remote repository.

Let us say you and your team are working on a website project, and you have made some changes to the code on your local computer. You want to upload those changes to the website's remote repository on GitHub so that the rest of the team can access them.

To do this, you use the `git push` command. It is like hitting the **Save** button on your code changes and uploading them to the remote repository for others to access:

```
PravinMishra@Pravin-MacBook-Pro ~ git push
Enumerating objects: 4, done.
Counting objects: 100% (4/4), done.
Delta compression using up to 8 threads
Compressing objects: 100% (3/3), done.
Writing objects: 100% (3/3), 332 bytes | 332.00 KiB/s, done.
Total 3 (delta 0), reused 0 (delta 0), pack-reused 0
To github.com:pravinmishra2907/the_cloudadvisory.git
   3c56719..2d2457d  main -> main
```

Figure 6.15: *Output of the command "git push"*

For example, let us say you made some changes to the `index.html` file in your local Git repository. To push those changes to the remote repository on GitHub, you navigate to your terminal or command prompt and use the following command: `git push origin master`:

```
PravinMishra@Pravin-MacBook-Pro ~ git push origin master
Enumerating objects: 4, done.
Counting objects: 100% (4/4), done.
Delta compression using up to 8 threads
Compressing objects: 100% (3/3), done.
Writing objects: 100% (3/3), 538 bytes | 538.00 KiB/s, done.
Total 3 (delta 0), reused 0 (delta 0), pack-reused 0
remote:
remote: Create a pull request for 'master' on GitHub by visiting:
remote:      https://github.com/pravinmishra2907/the_cloudadvisory/pull/new/master
remote:
To github.com:pravinmishra2907/the_cloudadvisory.git
 * [new branch]      master -> master
PravinMishra@Pravin-MacBook-Pro ~ 
```

Figure 6.16: *Output of the command "git push origin master "*

Here, `origin` is the name of the remote repository on GitHub, and `master` is the name of the branch you want to push your changes to. After running this command, your changes will be uploaded to the remote repository on GitHub.

Here, you can see the files from the local repository are successfully pushed to the remote repository.

To check if the files are successfully pushed to the remote repository or not, go to the GitHub remote repository, and refresh the web page. For example, the `index.html` and `style.css` are available here, as shown in *Figure 6.17*:

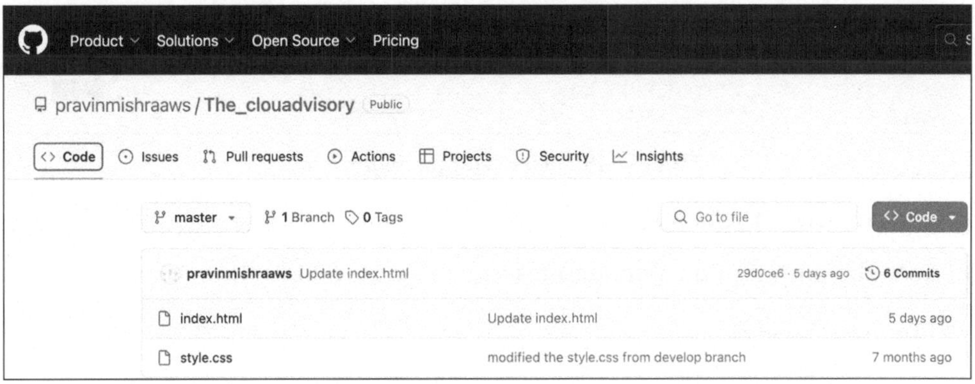

***Figure 6.17**: index.html and style.css files the GitHub remote repository*

This means that we successfully pushed the files from the local repository to the GitHub remote repository using the `git push` command.

We can also add new files, and update the code from the GitHub remote repository.

However, that file will not be available to the local repository, and to get that file to your local repository from the GitHub remote repository, you have to the `git pull` command.

Git Pull

`Git pull` is a command in Git that helps you update your local repository with the latest changes made to the code in a GitHub remote repository.

To use Git pull, you need to navigate to your local repository's directory using the terminal or command prompt, and then type the `git pull` command.

This command will download the latest changes to your local copy, and merge them with your local code. If there are any conflicts between your local code and the changes made by your team members, Git will notify you to resolve them.

After Git pull is complete, you can view the changes made from the GitHub remote repository in the local repository.

Overall, Git pull is an essential command for collaborative development, and helps keep all versions of the code in sync across different repositories.

Let us update our `index.html` from the GitHub remote repository.

Go to GitHub and select `index.html`.

Next, click **`Edit this file`**, and edit the code. Then, scroll down and commit message, as we commit message in Git:

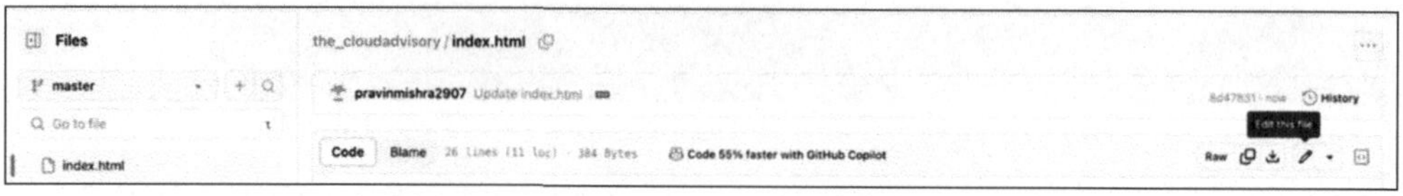

Figure 6.18: *Image "edit file index.html "*

Now, click on **`Commit changes`**.

Let us see the output of the commit message in *Figure 6.19*:

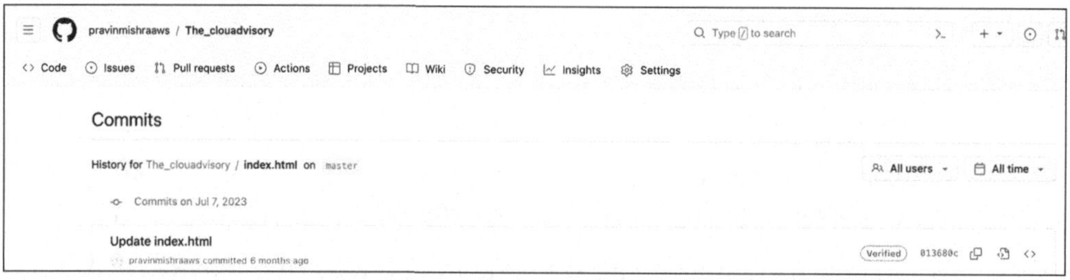

Figure 6.19: *Output of commit message*

In Git, to commit the changes, you have to perform some commands, but in GitHub, we can commit through just a few clicks.

Now, you have updated the index.html from the GitHub remote repository, but those changes are not available in our local repository code. We must also check this.

Instead of using any tool to make changes in the code, we will go to `index.html` file to make some changes in the code. To see the changes made in `index.html` file that go to your terminal, type out the **`git log`** command, which will show the changes that we have made in `index.html` file.

Open the `index.html`. Here, you can see that the code we added from the GitHub remote repository is not present. To get those changes in our local repository, we have to use the command `git pull`.

Go to the Terminal and run the command - `git pull origin master`.

Let us check the output of the preceding command, as shown in *Figure 6.20*:

```
PravinMishra@Pravin-MacBook-Pro ~ git pull origin master
remote: Enumerating objects: 5, done.
remote: Counting objects: 100% (5/5), done.
remote: Compressing objects: 100% (3/3), done.
remote: Total 3 (delta 1), reused 0 (delta 0), pack-reused 0
Unpacking objects: 100% (3/3), 778 bytes | 389.00 KiB/s, done.
From github.com:pravinmishra2907/the_cloudadvisory
 * branch            master     -> FETCH_HEAD
   40d6e3f..8d47831  master     -> origin/master
Updating 40d6e3f..8d47831
Fast-forward
 index.html | 9 ---------
 1 file changed, 9 deletions(-)
PravinMishra@Pravin-MacBook-Pro ~ █
```

Figure 6.20: *Output of the command "git pull origin master "*

Here you can see one file change, which means that the changes we made from the GitHub remote repository are now available in the local repository.

You can check these changes in your local repository.

Go to the `index.html` file that we have created already to make changes in that file. Here, you can see the changes are successfully pulled from the GitHub remote repository.

This is how you can pull the changes from a remote repository.

Now, suppose there is a GitHub repository which is already created by one of your team members which you want to get on your local system. This is where Git clone comes into the picture.

Git Clone

`git clone` is a command in Git that allows you to create a copy of a remote repository on your local computer. By using `git clone`, you can access the repository's code on your computer, make changes, and then upload those changes back to the remote repository. This is useful for collaborating with others on a project, or working on a website that is hosted on GitHub.

Suppose you want to work on a website that is hosted on GitHub, but you do not have a copy of the code on your local computer. To start working on the website, you will need to create a local copy of the website's code.

Let us say your teammate has stored the website code in the GitHub remote repository, and you want to get that code in your local computer to work on it.

To create a local copy of the GitHub repository, open your terminal or command prompt, and navigate to the directory on which you want to store the website's code.

Then, go to the GitHub repository for the website, click the green **`Code`** button, and from the dropdown, copy the repository's URL, as shown in *Figure 6.21*:

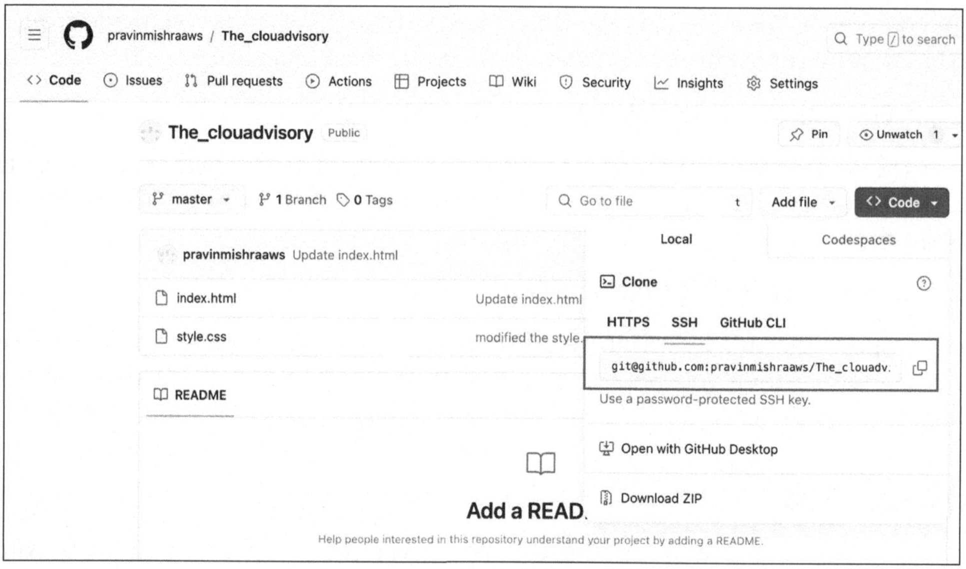

Figure 6.21: *Output of repository's URL*

In your terminal or command prompt, enter the command- `git clone <GitHub repository URL>`, and press *Enter.*

Let us see the output of the preceding command in *Figure 6.22*:

```
PravinMishra@Pravin-MacBook-Pro ~ git clone git@github.com:pravinmishra2907/the_cloudadvisory.git
Cloning into 'the_cloudadvisory'...
remote: Enumerating objects: 3, done.
remote: Counting objects: 100% (3/3), done.
remote: Compressing objects: 100% (2/2), done.
remote: Total 3 (delta 0), reused 0 (delta 0), pack-reused 0
Receiving objects: 100% (3/3), done.
```

Figure 6.22: *Output of the command "git clone <GitHub repository URL>"*

It will create a new directory in your local computer with the name of the GitHub repository, and download all the code files into that directory along with the entire history.

You can see it is successfully done.

Now perform the `ls` command in your terminal, and you can see a new directory is created with the name of the GitHub repository.

Enter this directory using the `cd` command.

Now that you are inside this directory, enter the `ls` command and press *Enter.*

Here, you can see all the code files from the GitHub repository are successfully copied to your local computer.

Now you can start making changes to the website's code by editing the files in the local copy.

When you are ready to share your changes with others or update the website's remote repository, you can use the `git push` command to upload your changes.

Overall, `git clone` is an essential command in Git that allows you to create a local copy of a remote repository. By cloning the repository, you can access and edit the code on your local computer.

In the next section, we will learn about the best practices to be followed by new GitHub users.

Tips and Best Practices for New GitHub Users

Starting on GitHub can be confusing because there is a lot of information, and many things that you can do. With years of experience in IT, I have learned some straightforward but effective practices for newcomers to GitHub. These practices are not just about getting the most out of GitHub, but about improving your skills as a developer and collaborator.

Commit Regularly

The essence of Git, and by extension GitHub, is version control. Version control, as you already know, is all about maintaining different versions of your code, and ensuring that you can travel back and view previous states of your project. The process of saving these different versions in Git parlance is called "**committing**."

Why is committing regularly so crucial?

First, it ensures that your **codebase remains updated**. Think of it as saving your progress in a video game. Every time you achieve a milestone, you save it so that you do not lose your progress. Similarly, when coding, as you complete features or fix bugs, you should commit your changes. This way, if something goes wrong in the future, you can always revert to a previous state.

Second, regular commits offer a clear history of your project. By glancing at the commit logs, anyone can understand the evolution of the project, the features added, the bugs fixed, and the general progression of the work. It is a narrative of your project's life, and frequent commits ensure this narrative is rich and detailed.

Clear Commit Messages

Let us talk about another vital aspect of committing: the commit messages. Now, when you save a document, you do not need to label it. However, imagine if you had hundreds of saved versions of that document. Would labels and descriptions not help identify each version?

Commit messages serve this exact purpose. They are descriptive labels that accompany each commit, giving insight into what was changed or added.

Writing clear and concise commit messages serves multiple purposes:

For Team Members

If you are working in a team, your colleagues will often look at commit messages to understand recent changes. A well-articulated message can save them time and prevent confusion.

For Your Future Self

When revisiting old projects, commit messages help understand the progression of the code. A clear message is like a note to your future self, ensuring you can pick up from where you left off.

For open-source Contributions

If you are contributing to open-source projects, those maintaining the project rely on commit messages to understand your contributions. A clear message can mean the difference between your chances of getting accepted or being overlooked.

Engage with the Community

GitHub is not just a tool, but a bustling community of developers. From novices to experts, from hobbyists to professionals, it is a melting pot of talent. One of the best things you can do as a new user is to engage with this community.

Learning

By participating in discussions, you expose yourself to new ideas, coding practices, and solutions. You get to see how other developers think and approach problems. This exposure can be incredibly beneficial in broadening your horizons.

Networking

Building a network is crucial in any profession. On GitHub, you get noticed by contributing to others' projects and being active in discussions. This can lead to collaborations, job opportunities, and even long-lasting professional relationships.

Feedback

By sharing your projects and asking for feedback, you open yourself up to constructive criticism. This feedback can be instrumental in improving your coding skills and enhancing your projects.

Some of the best learning experiences come from interacting with the developer community. It is a give-and-take, where you share your knowledge and, in return, absorb from others.

Understand `.gitignore`

When you are working on a project, not all files and folders need to be pushed to your repository. Some files, such as personal settings, huge data files, or system-generated files, are best left out. This is where `.gitignore` comes into play.

The `.gitignore` file is a simple text file that tells Git which files or directories to ignore in a project. It is a way to ensure that unnecessary or sensitive files do not end up in your repository.

Consider this: You are working on a Python project, and your system generates *a* `__pycache__` directory. This directory does not contain any code you have written, and it is not essential to the project. By adding `__pycache__/` to your `.gitignore` file, you ensure that Git ignores this directory, keeping your repo clean.

Another example is environment-specific configuration files that contain sensitive data, such as API keys. You would not want such information to be publicly accessible in your repository. Adding these files to `.gitignore` ensures they remain private.

A well-configured `.gitignore` file helps in maintaining a clean repository, ensures sensitive data remains private, and overall, enhances the quality of your projects on GitHub.

Remember, these practices are not just rules, but come from years of experience. Embracing them early on in your GitHub journey can set you up for success and make your journey smoother.

Key Terminologies

Repositories (or Repos)

In the vast universe of Git and GitHub, a 'repository' or 'repo' plays a fundamental role. Think of a repository as a big folder that holds together all the essential items related to a particular project. Just as you would organize your academic notes, papers, and handouts in different sections of a binder, a repository does something similar for your coding projects.

Inside this folder, there are multiple components: the actual source code, configuration files, documentation, graphics, and many other items, depending on the nature of the project. However, there is more to a repo than just being a place of storage. Unlike the static folders on your computer, a Git repository is dynamic. It is alive in the sense that it remembers. It remembers every change, every addition, every deletion that has happened over time. This memory is termed as the '**revision history**'. This history is crucial because it allows developers to view previous changes, and even revert to previous states if needed.

Each commit, which is a set of changes, adds a new page to this story.

Pull Requests (PRs)

Now, imagine you are working with a group of people on a collective assignment or project. You have been given a section to work on. Once you are done, you will want to merge your work with what others have done. This merging process is precisely where pull requests, commonly abbreviated as PRs, come into play in the world of GitHub.

When you believe your code or the changes you have made to a project are ready to be integrated into the main project, you create a pull request. It is like raising your hand in a classroom and saying, "*I have something to contribute.*" This PR serves as a request, asking those maintaining the project to review the changes you have proposed.

One of the most important aspects of PRs is the ability to discuss changes. You, as the contributor, can clarify your reasoning behind specific code modifications. Other collaborators, or those maintaining the project, can then review, suggest edits, or even praise good work. This iterative feedback loop ensures that the merged code is of the highest quality and aligns with the project's goals.

Issues

Have you ever been part of a group discussion or brainstorming session in which everyone shares their thoughts, points out problems, or suggests improvements? This dynamic is what '**Issues**' on GitHub aims to replicate. Issues are essentially discussion threads that anyone can start in a repository.

Issues can serve various purposes. They can be used to report bugs or problems in the code. They can highlight potential enhancements or new features that a contributor feels might be beneficial. They can also serve as a platform for asking questions related to the project's functionality or structure.

Effectively using issues can significantly improve a project's health. Having an open platform on which everyone, from seasoned developers to newbies, can voice their opinions and concerns, ensures that a project evolves holistically, considering diverse perspectives.

Forks

On GitHub, a fork is your personal copy of someone else's project. Just as you would photocopy a book to make annotations or highlights, forking allows you to have your version of a project on which you can experiment, make changes, or even take the project in a completely new direction, without affecting the original.

Forks are essential when you want to contribute to a project but do not have direct access to write on the main repository. After forking, you can make your changes in peace, and once you are satisfied, you can create a pull request, effectively saying, "*Hey, I've made these changes in my copy. Would you like to include them in the main project?*"

Forks give everyone the freedom to experiment, innovate, and contribute to projects they care about. You can use forked repositories to either learn from the code, make improvements, or sometimes tailor them for specific needs.

Conclusion

As we conclude this chapter, it is hoped that you now have a solid understanding of what GitHub is, and the immense value it brings to developers and teams across the globe. By grasping key terminologies and setting up your own account, you have taken the first crucial steps into a broader world of collaboration, version control, and open-source contribution. Whether it is through creating your first repository or learning the essential practices that will streamline your journey, these foundational skills set the stage for a productive and engaging experience with GitHub.

CHAPTER 7
Working Seamlessly With Both Git and GitHub

Introduction

In this chapter, we will explore the close and beneficial connection between Git, a strong distributed version control system, and GitHub, a platform that has changed the way developers collaborate. When these tools are used together, they make a powerful team for getting work done, and working together, making your coding efforts better in quality and efficiency. By the end of this chapter, you will have a good understanding and practical knowledge about the important parts of using Git and GitHub.

Structure

By the end of this chapter, we will have a deeper understanding of the following topics:

- Local and Remote repositories
- Best Practices for Collaborative Workflows
- Engaging with Hands-on Exercises and Real-World Scenarios

This chapter is designed to equip you with the skills and knowledge to seamlessly integrate Git with GitHub, enhancing your capabilities in both local and collaborative environments.

Integrating Local Repositories with GitHub

For many people, the journey starts on their personal computers, writing code in the comfort of their favourite text editors. This local safe place is where ideas are born.

However, to share these ideas with the world, we need to connect these local storage spaces to GitHub.

When starting with a local storage space, the first thing is to make sure that it has been set up with Git. If not, a simple `git init` in the main directory will do the job. Once our storage space is Git-ready, the next step is to make a new storage space on GitHub. Remember not to select the `Initialize this repository with a README` option unchecked, as we are linking an existing repository.

With the GitHub repository ready, go back to your terminal or command prompt. Here, you will link your local repository to GitHub using the following command:

```
git remote add origin [your-repository-url]
```

Replace `[your-repository-url]` with the URL of your GitHub repository. Now, your local and remote repositories are linked! Pushing and pulling changes becomes easy from this point onwards.

In the previous chapter, we learned about how to create a remote repository, and then how to link a remote repository with the local repository. We have also understood Git pull, push and how to clone the repository.

In the next section, let us understand some other important Git commands.

Collaborative Workflows

Whether working with a small group of developers, or in a big tech environment, learning how to have a smooth way of working is always important. GitHub is great for this kind of teamwork. It has changed how developers work together, providing tools and practices such as forks, pull requests, and code reviews that are really important for keeping things working well.

Let us take a closer look at what these practices involve, and how they make working together easier.

The First Step: Fork

Imagine you come across an open-source project on GitHub that is almost perfect for your needs, However, you see room for improvement or customization. By forking this project, you create your own copy, giving you the freedom to experiment and make changes without affecting the original.

Let us understand this with an example.

Imagine there is a developer, Alex, who discovers a blogging platform project on GitHub. Alex sees potential for a feature that allows for enhanced image galleries. By forking the project, Alex can work on this feature independently, testing and refining it in their own repository.

Bridging Contributions: Pull Requests

Once you have made improvements or added features in your forked repository, you will likely want to share these enhancements with the original project. This is where pull requests come into play. They allow you to propose your changes to the original repository, inviting review and discussion.

Now, continuing with the previous example, after implementing the image gallery feature, Alex is ready to contribute it back to the original project. Alex opens a pull request, effectively saying, "*I've added this feature, and I believe it could be valuable to your project.*" This pull request initiates a dialogue between Alex and the original manager of the project.

Ensuring Quality: Code Reviews

Before Alex's changes are merged into the main project, they must undergo a code review. This process ensures that contributions maintain the project's quality and coherence. Code reviews are a collaborative forum for feedback, suggestions, and learning.

Now, let us go back to the example in which Alex has sent a pull request. During the review of Alex's pull request, another developer, Jordan, suggests improvements to the feature's code, making it more efficient and compatible with the project's existing structure. Alex learns from Jordan's expertise, enhancing his skill set, and contributing a refined feature to the project.

The Seamless Workflow

The journey from forking to pull requests to code reviews embodies the spirit of collaborative development. It begins with the initiative of an individual, transitions through community engagement and dialogue, and culminates in the collective enhancement of the project.

Why This Workflow Matters

For developers like Alex and Jordan, GitHub's collaborative tools provide a structured yet flexible framework for contributing to projects. Whether you are adding a new feature, fixing a bug, or improving documentation, this workflow ensures that every contribution is carefully considered and reviewed, enhancing the project's overall quality and utility.

The Power of Collaboration

GitHub, with features such as forking, pull requests, and code reviews, is more than just platform with a series of associated steps, but the manifestation of a community-driven development process, fostering a culture of openness, learning, and mutual respect among developers. By engaging with these practices, you not only contribute to the projects you care about but also become part of a global community of creators, building better software together.

Practical Exercises or Case Studies for Using Git and GitHub in Unison

We will now go into practical exercises and real-world examples that show us how to use Git and GitHub well. This is where you should undertake some independent exercises to solidify your knowledge.

By the end of this section, you should understand how to move around both platforms easily, making your coding and teamwork skills better.

Exercise 1: Establishing Your Repository and Mastering Basic Commands

Objective:

This exercise aims to familiarize you with setting up a repository on your local machine, connecting it to GitHub, and using essential Git commands to manage your code.

Let's repeat all the steps we have done in the previous chapter, such as creating a local repository and remote repository, and linking them together. Then, use commands such as status, checkout, branch, merge, pull, and push.

Setting Up Your Environment

Ensure that Git is installed on your computer. If it is not, download and install it from the official Git website. You will also need a GitHub account. If you have not got one, visit GitHub's website to sign up.

Creating a Local Repository

Open your Terminal or command prompt. Navigate to the folder where you want to create your repository using the `cd` command. Run `git init` to initialize a new Git repository.

Making Changes and Committing

Create a new file in your repository, or make changes to an existing one. Run `git add` to stage your changes, and `git commit -m "Your commit message"` to commit the changes.

Connecting to GitHub

Go to GitHub and create a new repository. Copy the repository's URL. Back in your terminal, run `git remote add origin your-repository-url`. This links your local repository to GitHub.

Pushing to GitHub

Run `git push -u origin master` to push your changes to GitHub. If prompted, enter your GitHub username and password.

Learning Outcomes

This exercise teaches you the essentials of version control and how to synchronize your local repository with GitHub, ensuring your code is safely stored and accessible from anywhere.

Exercise 2: Contributing to Open Source

Embracing Open Source

Open-source projects are a fantastic way to contribute to the larger developer community. They offer a chance to learn, share knowledge, and improve the tools and systems we all rely on.

Finding a Project

Visit GitHub and find an open-source project you are interested in. Look for issues tagged with "*good first issue*" or "*help wanted.*"

Forking and Cloning

Fork the repository to your own GitHub account. This creates a copy that you have full control over. Clone the repository to your local machine using `git clone your-forked-repo-url`.

Making Changes

Create a new branch using `git checkout -b your-branch-name`. Make your changes, or fix the issue. Run `git add .` and `git commit -m "Your commit message"`.

Creating a Pull Request

Push your changes to your forked repository on GitHub with `git push origin your-`

`branch-name`. Go to the original repository on GitHub. You should see an option to **`Compare & pull request`**. Click it, fill in the description, and create the pull request.

Learning Outcomes

This exercise introduces you to the world of open-source contributions, teaching you how to navigate repositories, make changes, and submit pull requests.

Case Study: Global Team Collaboration

Imagine a scenario in which a software development team is spread across three continents. The team is working on a web application with a tight deadline.

Overcoming Time Zones with Git and GitHub

Git's distributed nature allows each team member to work locally on their own schedule, while GitHub's collaborative features enable the seamless integration of everyone's work.

Forking and Branching

Each team member forks the main repository and creates feature-specific branches for their tasks. This ensures that everyone's work is isolated, and can be reviewed independently.

Continuous Integration and Deployment

The team utilizes GitHub Actions to automate testing and deployment. Every pull request triggers a series of automated tests, ensuring that any new code does not break existing functionality.

Code Reviews and Collaboration

Pull requests are used for code reviews. Team members from different time zones can leave comments, suggest changes, and approve the work. This asynchronous method of communication ensures that no one is left waiting, and work continues around the clock.

Conflict Resolution and Merging

Occasionally, merge conflicts occur. However, because of Git's powerful merging capabilities and GitHub's user-friendly interface, resolving conflicts is easy. The team is able to keep the codebase consistent and up to date.

Learning Outcomes

This example shows how Git and GitHub really work together in a team, making it easier to work at different times, improving the quality of the code, and making development smoother.

By doing these activities and thinking about this example, you should now know how to use Git and GitHub together for successful teamwork in coding.

Conclusion

One thing you realize when you learn about Git and GitHub is that coding is not just something you do alone, but something we all do together. Every time you suggest a change or bring up a problem on GitHub, you are adding to the bigger picture of making software. You are not just someone who writes the code, but part of a larger team, an important part of a group that believes in sharing knowledge and making impactful software.

As we keep moving forward, armed with the knowledge and skills we have gained, remember that becoming skilled in Git and GitHub goes beyond just memorizing commands or following steps. It is about grasping the idea behind version control, the teamwork aspect of development, and the power of community support. Each Git command and GitHub action is a step towards improving your abilities as a developer, collaborator, and contributor.

In the next chapter, we will build on what you have learned in the previous chapters. You will learn about the details of handling large-scale repositories, using advanced merging strategies, and making the most of Git's scripting abilities to automate your workflow like never before. Get ready to enhance your expertise as we continue to unleash the full potential of Git.

CHAPTER 8
Advanced Git Techniques

Introduction

In this chapter, we will explore advanced techniques in Git. Mastering Git involves knowing when and how to use its advanced features. The many commands and choices in Git might feel like a lot, especially for those who are new to it. However, with proper help, figuring out Git becomes easier and even fun.

By the end of this chapter, you will grasp advanced Git techniques. The chapter aims to give you advanced essential topic knowledge and ensure that you can deal with tricky situations, make your work smoother, and contribute well to projects.

Structure

By the end of this chapter, you will have a deeper understanding of:

- Rebase versus Merge
- Interactive Rebasing
- Cherry-picking
- Bisect
- Stashing
- Reflog
- Submodules
- Worktrees
- Advanced Configuration and Aliases
- Hooks
- Large File Storage with Git LFS

So, let us get started. We will explore advanced Git techniques, unlocking the full potential of this powerful tool and transforming your workflow.

Rebase versus Merge

While `rebase` and `merge` may seem to serve similar purposes at first glance, understanding the differences in when and how to use each can significantly impact your project's history and workflow.

Diving Deep into Merge

Let us start by looking at `merge`. Merging is one of the most common operations in Git. It takes the contents of a source branch and integrates it with the target branch. In doing so, it preserves the history of both branches, creating a new commit in the process. This commit has two parent commits, each pointing to the tip of the merged branches.

Real-Life Example of Merge

Consider a scenario where you are working on a new feature in a dedicated branch while your teammate is fixing a bug in another branch. Once both tasks are completed, you want to bring these changes together. This is where `merge` shines. By merging, you create a tangible link between these two lines of development. This not only maintains a record of when the changes were brought together but also preserves the context in which they were developed.

Implications of Using Merge

While `merge` is a safe option, it does come with its own set of implications. One of the most noticeable is the potentially cluttered commit history it can create, especially in a busy project with lots of branches. Every merge results in a new commit, and if merges are frequent, your history can become a dense network of intertwining branches, making it harder to follow the history of specific changes.

Exploring Rebase

On the flip side, we have `rebase`. If `merge` is like creating a junction in your project's history, `rebase` is like a fast-forward. It takes a set of commits and applies them to a new base. This results in a much cleaner, linear commit history, as it avoids the creation of additional merge commits.

An Example Using Rebase

Imagine that you have been working on a feature in a branch, and in the meantime, several commits have been added to the main branch. Instead of creating a `merge` `commit` to bring these changes together, you can `rebase` your feature branch onto the main branch. This moves your entire feature branch to sit on top of the current state of the main branch, creating a cleaner, more readable history.

When to Use Rebase Carefully

However, `rebase` is not without its complications. It essentially rewrites commit history, which can be dangerous, especially when working with shared branches. If you rebase commits that are already pushed to a shared repository and then push the rebased branch, you risk creating confusion and potential conflicts for your teammates. It is crucial to only rebase commits that are local and not shared with others to avoid these issues.

Weighing the Pros and Cons

Both `merge` and `rebase` have their place in Git's toolkit. `Merge` is straightforward, preserves history, and is safe to use in shared branches. `Rebase` creates a clean, linear history, but requires caution and understanding of its implications. It is like choosing between two paths in a forest; one is well-trodden and easy to follow but may take longer to traverse (`merge`). The other is more direct and can get you to your destination quicker but requires careful navigation to avoid getting lost (`rebase`).

Conclusion and Best Practices

Understanding the balance between `rebase` and `merge`, and knowing when to use each, is crucial for maintaining sanity in your commit history. `Merge` should be your go-to strategy for shared branches, particularly when you want to preserve the context of parallel development. It allows you to combine histories while maintaining the integrity of your timeline.

On the other hand, `rebase` is ideal for local branches where you seek a clean, linear history. It is especially useful in product development scenarios where your base product is being customized for different clients. Imagine that you have a product with a core set of features (main branch), and for each client, you develop custom features (client-feature branch) on top of the base product. Before delivering the custom product, you would rebase the client-feature branch onto the updated main branch to integrate all the new features and improvements from the base product without cluttering the history with merge commits. This keeps the custom feature branch up-to-date and ensures that the history is linear and clean, which simplifies both understanding and debugging.

Well, maybe this sounds complex, but do not worry. Let me explain this in detail.

Interactive Rebasing

Over many years of working in the IT sector, the real importance of keeping a well-organized and clear commit history in any Git repository has become clear. It is not just about making things look neat and tidy; it is about creating a clear story of the changes, fixes, and improvements made to the code over time. This is where interactive rebasing, a feature in Git, becomes a very useful tool for any developer, no matter how much experience they have.

Understanding Interactive Rebasing

Interactive rebasing can be best described as a fine-tuning process for your commit history. Imagine that you have been working on a feature branch for several days, making commits as you progress. You might have a commit history that looks a bit messy with messages like `fix typo`, `remove extra space`, `update function X`, and so on. In a professional setting, especially when working in large teams or on open-source projects, having such a chaotic commit history can make it incredibly difficult for your peers to understand the evolution of your code.

This is where interactive rebasing shines. It enables you to rewrite your commit history, providing options to reword commit messages, squash multiple trivial commits into a single commit, reorder commits, or even remove unnecessary commits. This way, you make a clearer, more logical order of changes that shows how your feature developed.

Rewording Commit Messages

Let us start with rewording commit messages. We have all been there – hastily typing out a commit message only to realize moments later that it is filled with typos or it is not descriptive enough. Interactive rebasing allows you to go back and rewrite those commit messages.

Imagine you are working on a new authentication feature for a web application. You made a commit with the message `add login function`.

Did you notice the error?

With interactive rebasing, you can easily correct this to `add login function`, ensuring that your commit history is free from such errors.

Squashing Trivial Commits

Next, let us talk about squashing trivial commits. During development, you might find yourself making a series of small, incremental changes – and that is completely fine. However, these do not need to be reflected as individual commits in your history. For example, if you have commits like `fix typo in function X`, `add null check`, and `update comments`, these could all be squashed into a single commit with a message like `improve function X's robustness and documentation`.

This not only cleans up your commit history but also makes it easier for others (and yourself) to understand the evolution of your code. It helps in isolating specific changes, making it simpler to identify when a particular bug was introduced or when a specific feature was implemented.

Dropping Unwanted Changes

Sometimes, while coding, you might find that you have made a commit that, in hindsight, was not necessary. Maybe it was a quick solution or a change that got replaced by newer updates. With interactive rebasing, you have the power to remove such commits from your history, ensuring that only relevant changes are preserved.

Consider a scenario where you were trying to fix a bug, and you made several commits as you experimented with different solutions. When you find the right solution and add it, those earlier trial changes are no longer needed. Interactive rebasing helps you remove them from your history, making everything neat and focused.

Reordering Commits for Logical Flow

Maintaining a logical flow of commits is crucial, especially when you are working on complex features or bug fixes. Sometimes, you might realize that a commit you made earlier should actually come later in the sequence, or vice versa. Interactive rebasing provides you with the capability to reorder your commits to create a more logical and understandable sequence of changes.

Imagine you are working on a feature that needs changes in both the backend and frontend of an application. Ideally, you would prefer to commit all backend changes first and then the frontend ones. However, during development, you might mix up these commits. Interactive rebasing helps you rearrange them so that backend commits come first, followed by the frontend ones. This makes it simpler for any developer checking your code to follow the order of changes.

Practical Examples and Use Cases

To put things into a real-world context, let us consider a practical example.

Imagine you are contributing to a popular open-source project on GitHub. Open-source maintainers usually prefer a clean and clear commit history for any pull requests they receive, as it makes code review more straightforward and helps in maintaining the project's overall quality.

You have worked hard on your feature, made several commits, but your commit history is a bit chaotic. By using interactive rebasing, you can clean up your commits, squash trivial changes, reword any unclear commit messages, and reorder commits for a logical flow. Once you have done this, your pull request stands a much better chance of being accepted because you have made the maintainer's job easier – they can clearly see each step you took in your development process and understand the rationale behind each change.

Interactive rebasing provides clarity, coherence, and a clean record of the evolution of your code. It is a tool that demands respect and attention, as misusing it (especially on shared branches) can lead to complications. However, when used correctly, it becomes an indispensable part of your Git toolkit, enhancing collaboration and understanding within your team.

By adopting interactive rebasing as a regular part of your workflow, you are not just cleaning up your commit history; you are creating a clear, understandable, and valuable record of your development process. This, in the long run, saves time, reduces confusion, and improves the overall quality of your code. And that, as any seasoned developer will tell you, is worth its weight in gold.

Cherry-Picking in Git

Cherry-picking in Git can be understood as a surgical tool; **it is precise and meant for specific tasks**. When you cherry-pick a commit, you are essentially selecting a single commit from a branch and applying it onto another branch. It is like being in a garden filled with various fruit-bearing trees **(branches)**, and you have the ability to pick a particular fruit **(commit)** from one tree and graft it onto another tree. It is a way of saying, "**I want this specific change and not the rest.**"

This process might seem simple, but it has details and possible issues, especially when the branches have gone in different directions. The commit you are picking has its own history, changes, and context that may or may not work well with the branch you are putting it on. It is not just about changing the code; it is about how that change works with the existing code in the branch you are putting it on.

Use Cases for Cherry-Picking

Cherry-picking is a handy technique in Git that has several practical applications:

Applying Hotfixes

One of the most common use cases for cherry-picking is applying hotfixes. Consider a scenario where your team is working on a big feature in a separate branch, and suddenly, a critical bug is discovered in production. The feature branch has a commit that fixes this bug, but it is intertwined with other commits related to the feature, which are not ready for production.

In such cases, creating a hotfix branch from the main branch and using git cherry-pick to apply just the commit that fixes the bug is the way to go. This ensures that the bug is fixed in production without deploying the incomplete feature.

Managing Multiple Code Branches

Working with multiple code branches is another scenario where cherry-picking shines. Let us say you have a develop branch, a feature-A branch, and a feature-B branch. A commit in feature-A solves a bug that is also present in feature-B. Instead of merging the entire feature-A into feature-B, which might bring in unwanted changes, you can simply cherry-pick the specific commit that fixes the bug, ensuring clean and relevant commit history in feature-B.

Step-by-Step Guide to Cherry-Pick

Let us walk through the process of cherry-picking a commit. Assume that you have a commit with a hash `abc123` in branch feature-A that you want to apply to branch feature-B:

1. First, ensure that you have the latest changes in your repository:

   ```
   git pull origin feature-B
   ```

2. Switch to the branch you want to apply the commit to:

   ```
   git checkout feature-B
   ```

3. Use the `cherry-pick` command:

   ```
   git cherry-pick abc123
   ```

Now, You can check how we switched to another branch using `git checkout` command, as shown in *Figure* 8.1:

```
(venv) PravinMishra@Pravin-MacBook-Pro ~ git checkout feature-B
Switched to branch 'feature-B'
(venv) PravinMishra@Pravin-MacBook-Pro ~ git cherry-pick d6d3f792d3c9739c6706770459420645640fedd9
[feature-B 4373370] Added a dummy commit in feature-A
 Date: Tue Dec 5 16:21:39 2023 +0530
 1 file changed, 1 insertion(+), 1 deletion(-)
```

Figure 8.1: *Output of the command " git checkout feature-B "*

4. If there are no conflicts, Git will apply the commit directly. If there are conflicts, Git will pause and allow you to resolve them before completing the cherry-pick.

Resolving Conflicts

Conflicts during cherry-picking are common, especially when the commit you are applying has changes that are not compatible with the branch you are applying it to. In such cases, Git will highlight the conflicts and ask you to resolve them manually. Once resolved, you can continue the cherry-pick process by running:

```
git cherry-pick --continue
```

Real-Time Example: Fixing a Bug Across Features

Let us consider a real-world example. There was a project with two different parts, one for logging in (feature-login) and another for signing up (feature-signup). Both parts were being worked on at the same time. We found a mistake in how users were being checked, something both parts needed. A team member fixed the mistake in the logging in part. Instead of waiting for the logging in part to be added to the main part and then fixing the signing up part, we simply took the fixed mistake from the logging in part and added it to the signing up part. This way, both parts could keep going without any problems, and the mistake was fixed in both.

Best Practices and Tips

Here are some good ways to handle code changes:

Commit Atomicity

Ensure that your commits are atomic, meaning they represent a single logical change. This makes cherry-picking easier and cleaner, as you can pick exactly what you need without bringing in unrelated changes.

Clear Commit Messages

Write clear and descriptive commit messages. When cherry-picking, you might be looking through a long list of commit hashes, and clear messages make it easier to identify the commit you need.

Test After Cherry-Picking

Always test your code after cherry-picking. Even if the cherry-pick process does not result in conflicts, it is crucial to ensure that the changes work as expected in the new branch.

Cherry-picking is an incredibly useful tool in Git's arsenal, allowing for precise control over what changes are applied to your branches. It is especially valuable when dealing with hotfixes and managing changes across multiple code branches. By following best practices, understanding when to use it, and being mindful of potential conflicts, you can leverage cherry-picking to streamline your workflow, maintain clean commit histories, and ensure that your codebase is always in the best possible state.

By mastering the art of cherry-picking, you equip yourself with the ability to navigate complex development workflows with ease.

Utilizing Git Bisect to Pinpoint Bugs

Often, you might find yourself introduced to a bug that is causing disaster in your application, and pinpointing the exact commit that caused this issue becomes crucial. Now, this could be compared to finding a needle in a haystack, especially if you are working with a large and extensive commit history. Here, Git introduces a brilliant feature named '*bisect*' that plays the role of a detective in our coding storyline.

The Power of Git Bisect

Git bisect uses a **binary search algorithm** to swiftly and efficiently find the commit that introduced a change in behavior in your code – whether that is a bug, a performance issue, or any other unexpected change. The beauty of Git bisect lies in its simplicity and efficiency. Instead of manually looking through each and every commit to find where things went wrong, which can be extremely time-consuming and error-prone, Git bisect automates this process, reducing the number of steps needed to find the problematic commit.

Let us use a real-world scenario to better illustrate this: imagine you are working on a large-scale web application, and you recently noticed a critical bug that is causing a certain feature to malfunction. This feature was working perfectly fine two weeks ago, but now, it is not. You have hundreds of commits between now and two weeks ago. Manually checking each commit would not only be impractical but could also drive anyone to the brink of frustration.

The Process of Bisecting

Imagine you are developing a web application, and you have recently discovered a bug that affects the login functionality. This bug was not present two weeks ago, but with daily commits from multiple team members, identifying the problematic commit seems daunting.

Step 1: Start the Bisect Process

First, you need to start bisecting. Open your Terminal, navigate to your project directory, and start Git bisect mode by running:

```
git bisect start
```

Step 2: Mark the Bad Commit

Mark the current state of your project (where the bug is present) as `bad`. If you are on the commit where the bug is noticed, you can simply do:

```
git bisect bad
```

Step 3: Mark the Good Commit

Next, mark a commit where you are sure everything was working fine. If you know the bug was not present two weeks ago, find a commit from that period and mark it as `good`. You can use git log to find an old commit hash.

Let us say the hash is 297c1e5a4c20e4a77a09bc364b8f290e5aafbd9a:

```
git bisect good 5cbdf045c5c078dcee52095d45a14a0df8223d1b
```

Step 4: Narrow Down the Commits

`git bisect` will now checkout a commit halfway between the `good` and `bad` commits. Test your application to see if the bug is present. If the bug is present, mark the commit as `bad`; if not, mark it as `good`. This process will guide `git bisect` in which direction to continue the search.

If the bug is present:

```
git bisect bad
```

If the bug is not present:

```
git bisect good
```

Step 5: Repeat Testing

Repeat *Step* 4. Each time you mark a commit as `good` or `bad`, `git bisect` will check out another commit based on the binary search algorithm. Continue testing and marking commits until `git bisect` pinpoints the exact commit that introduced the bug.

Step 6: Identifying the Culprit

Once Git bisect has found the problematic commit, it will output something like:

```
PravinMishra@Pravin-MacBook-Pro~ git bisect good

8d6518d2ef6a354dc745380d42e5980b5517ccdf is the first bad commit
```

```
commit 8d6518d2ef6a354dc745380d42e5980b5517ccdf
Author: Pravin Mishra <hello@pravinmishra.in>
Date:   Sat Mar 16 11:37:09 2024 +0200
    changed VPC CIDR
 vpc/vpc.yaml | 2 +-
 1 file changed, 1 insertion(+), 1 deletion(-)
```

Now you have identified the commit that introduced the bug. You can investigate the changes made in this commit to understand what went wrong.

Step 7: Exiting Bisect Mode

After you have identified the problematic commit, exit bisect mode and return to your original branch (for example, main or master) by running:

```
git bisect reset
```

This command will end the bisect session and bring you back to the starting point.

This small example illustrates how Git bisect can save time and frustration when tracking down bugs. Remember, the effectiveness of Git bisect significantly depends on having a clear and structured commit history.

The Importance of a Good Commit History

This brings us to another crucial point – the importance of maintaining a clean and meaningful commit history. When using Git bisect, having a chaotic commit history can make the process more complicated than it needs to be. On the contrary, a well-maintained commit history, with meaningful commit messages and atomic commits (each commit representing a single logical change), can make the process of finding bugs with Git bisect easy.

Troubleshooting and Tips for Effective Bisecting

However, like any other tool, Git bisect has its challenges. Sometimes, the issue is not easy to reproduce, or the behavior change is not clear. In these cases, using scripts or extra debugging tools along with Git bisect can be really helpful.

It is also important to make sure that every commit in your history can be built. Testing a commit that does not build or run will give wrong results. Remember, Git bisect works best when the change in behavior is clear and can be reproduced.

Git bisect is a vital tool for developers. It saves time on frustrating debugging, making the process more efficient and accurate. It helps keep your codebase in good shape and ensures that bugs can be found and fixed quickly. So, use Git bisect and make bug hunting a journey of efficient debugging and learning.

Stashing: A Lifesaver in Your Git Workflow

Imagine, you are in the middle of writing code for a new feature on your feature branch. The code is halfway done and certainly not ready for a commit. Suddenly, a team member reports a critical bug in the master branch that needs immediate attention. What do you do with your uncommitted changes? You cannot commit them because they are incomplete, and you cannot discard them because you need them later. This is where `git stash` comes into play, offering a seamless solution to save your changes temporarily, allowing you to switch branches, and address urgent issues.

Understanding Git Stash

Git stash acts like a clipboard for your changes, where you can cut your changes from your working directory and paste them back when you are ready. It stashes away your modifications, reverting your working directory to the last commit, yet keeping your changes safe for later use.

Let's learn these commands: Stash, Apply, and Pop.

Creating a Stash

The basic command `git stash` takes your uncommitted changes, both staged and unstaged, and saves them in a new stash.

Now, the output of the command `git stash` is shown in *Figure* 8.2:

```
(venv) PravinMishra@Pravin-MacBook-Pro ~ git stash
Saved working directory and index state WIP on feature-B: 4373370 Added a dummy commit in feature-A
```

***Figure* 8.2**: *Output of the command " git stash "*

Applying a Stash

`git stash apply` restores the changes saved in the latest stash, but it does not remove the stash from the list of stashes. You can continue to apply it as many times as you need.

Now, the output of the command `git apply` is shown in *Figure* 8.3:

```
(venv) PravinMishra@Pravin-MacBook-Pro ~ git diff
(venv) PravinMishra@Pravin-MacBook-Pro ~ git stash apply
On branch feature-B
Changes not staged for commit:
  (use "git add <file>..." to update what will be committed)
  (use "git restore <file>..." to discard changes in working directory)
        modified:   index.html

no changes added to commit (use "git add" and/or "git commit -a")
```

***Figure 8.3**: Output of the command " git apply "*

Popping a Stash

`git stash pop`, on the other hand, applies the stash and then removes it from the stash list, making sure your stash list stays clean.

Now, the output of the command `git stash pop` is shown in *Figure* 8.4:

```
(venv) PravinMishra@Pravin-MacBook-Pro ~ git diff
(venv) PravinMishra@Pravin-MacBook-Pro ~ git stash pop
On branch feature-B
Changes not staged for commit:
  (use "git add <file>..." to update what will be committed)
  (use "git restore <file>..." to discard changes in working directory)
        modified:   index.html

no changes added to commit (use "git add" and/or "git commit -a")
Dropped refs/stash@{0} (03b709c8bab9632250f79f670bcad23f9fea0a9d)
```

***Figure 8.4**: Output of the command git stash pop*

Managing Multiple Stashes

You might find yourself in a situation where you have multiple stashes. Each stash is stored with a unique identifier. You can view the list of all your stashes with the `git stash list` and apply a specific stash using `git stash apply stash@{n}` where n is the identifier of the stash.

Now, the output of the command `git stash list` is shown in *Figure* 8.5:

```
(venv) PravinMishra@Pravin-MacBook-Pro ~ git stash list
stash@{0}: On feature-B: Updated index.html file, but update is not complete yet
stash@{1}: WIP on feature-B: 4373370 Added a dummy commit in feature-A
stash@{2}: WIP on feature-B: 4373370 Added a dummy commit in feature-A
```

***Figure 8.5**: Output of the command git stash list*

Cleaning Up: Dropping Stashes

To remove a specific stash, you can use `git stash drop stash@{n}`.

Now, the output of command `git stash drop stash@{n}` is shown in *Figure* 8.6:

```
(venv) PravinMishra@Pravin-MacBook-Pro ~ git stash drop stash@{0}
Dropped stash@{0} (45a2b81e9d46400de96d1d20bf398abedc4b5080)
```

Figure 8.6: *Output of the command " git stash drop stash@{n}"*

And to clear all your stashes, `git stash clear` is the command you need.

Now, the output command of `git stash clear` is shown in *Figure* 8.7:

```
(venv) PravinMishra@Pravin-MacBook-Pro ~ git stash clear
(venv) PravinMishra@Pravin-MacBook-Pro ~ git stash list
```

Figure 8.7: *Output of the command " git stash clear "*

Stashing Untracked and Ignored Files

By default, `git stash` does not stash untracked or ignored files. If you want to include untracked files in your stash, you can use `git stash -u`. To include ignored and untracked files, `git stash -a` is the command to use.

A Use Case: Feature Branch Workflow

In a feature branch workflow, developers often work on different features simultaneously, leading to frequent context switching. git stash proves to be invaluable in such workflows, allowing developers to save their changes on one feature branch, switch to another feature branch to make quick edits, and then switch back and retrieve their stashed changes.

Tips for Effective Stashing

Here are some simple tips to stash changes effectively in Git:

Stash with a Message

Using `git stash save "message"` allows you to add a descriptive message to your stash, making it easier to identify later.

Now, the output command of `git stash save "message"` is shown in *Figure* 8.8:

```
(venv) PravinMishra@Pravin-MacBook-Pro ~ git stash save "Updated index.html file, but update is not complete yet"
Saved working directory and index state On feature-B: Updated index.html file, but update is not complete yet
```

Figure 8.8: *Output of the command "git stash save "message"*

Be Mindful of Stashed Changes

Remember to apply your stashed changes before making additional changes to avoid merge conflicts.

Regular Housekeeping

Periodically go through your stash list and clear out stashes that are no longer needed.

Troubleshooting Common Stashing Issues

Let us talk about common issues you might face when using stash in Git. Stashing is a handy tool, but sometimes things can go a bit haywire. Here, we will cover two common problems – stash conflicts and lost stashes. If you ever find yourself scratching your head over these issues, worry not – we have solutions for you.

Stash Conflicts

When applying a stash, you might run into conflicts. This happens when the code in the stash does not merge cleanly with the code in your working directory. In such cases, treat it as a merge conflict, resolve the conflicts, and continue with your work.

Lost Stashes

If you accidentally drop a stash, you might think it is gone forever. However, `git fsck --unreachable | grep commit` can help you find commits that are no longer reachable, and you might be able to rescue your lost stash.

Stashing provides flexibility and enhances workflow efficiency. By mastering `git stash`, you can juggle multiple tasks at once, maintain a clean working directory, and ensure that you are always ready to address urgent issues without losing your progress on ongoing tasks. With the tips, tricks, and troubleshooting advice provided in this section, you are well-equipped to make the most out of this powerful feature.

Reflog: Safeguarding Your Work with Git's Safety Net

`Git reflog` is essentially a ledger, a meticulous record-keeper of every movement within your Git repository. It logs each action you have taken, every commit, every branch switch, and even those moments when you think all is lost because you have accidentally deleted a branch or force-pushed the wrong changes. In simple terms, it is the safety net of Git, ensuring that no piece of your work gets lost in the vast expanse of your repository.

The Power of Git Reflog in Action

Imagine, you have been working really hard on a feature branch, making changes step by step. You decide to tidy up your record of changes, and in a moment of too much excitement, you push your changes forcefully. You realize you sent your changes to the wrong branch, and all your carefully made changes seem to be gone.

In any ordinary scenario, this could mean hours of work lost and a significant loss to your progress. But with `git reflog`, it is merely a minor setback. By typing `git reflog`, a list appears on your screen, showing every action you have taken, each associated with a unique reference.

Now, the output command of `git reflog` is shown in *Figure* 8.9:

```
(venv) PravinMishra@Pravin-MacBook-Pro ~ git reflog
4373370 (HEAD -> feature-B) HEAD@{0}: reset: moving to HEAD
4373370 (HEAD -> feature-B) HEAD@{1}: reset: moving to HEAD
4373370 (HEAD -> feature-B) HEAD@{2}: reset: moving to HEAD
4373370 (HEAD -> feature-B) HEAD@{3}: cherry-pick: Added a dummy commit in feature-A
8d47831 (origin/master, master) HEAD@{4}: checkout: moving from feature-A to feature-B
de95a5f (feature-A) HEAD@{5}: checkout: moving from feature-B to feature-A
8d47831 (origin/master, master) HEAD@{6}: checkout: moving from feature-A to feature-B
de95a5f (feature-A) HEAD@{7}: commit: Added another dummy commit to feature-A
d6d3f79 HEAD@{8}: commit: Added a dummy commit in feature-A
8d47831 (origin/master, master) HEAD@{9}: checkout: moving from master to feature-A
8d47831 (origin/master, master) HEAD@{10}: checkout: moving from feature-B to master
```

Figure 8.9: *Output of the command git reflog*

With a simple `git reset --hard <reference>`, you get back your lost work, bringing back the changes like they never disappeared.

The Mechanics of Git Reflog

Understanding how `git reflog` works is important to see its power. Whenever you do something in Git, like making a commit, changing branches, or doing a rebase, `git reflog` keeps a record. Each record in this log is linked to a `HEAD` reference, which points to a certain commit in your Git history.

The great thing about `git reflog` is that it is simple and works quietly in the background. You do not need to do anything; it automatically keeps track of every action to make sure nothing gets lost.

Real-Time Examples and Use Cases

Let us look into some real-time examples to solidify our understanding of `git reflog`.

Case 1: Recovering Lost Commits

Imagine you are working on a critical bug fix, and you have just made a series of commits addressing the issue. In your haste to clean up your commit history, you decide to squash your commits. But something goes wrong, and your commits disappear.

With `git reflog`, you navigate back through your history and find the reference to your lost commits, and with a `git reset --hard <reference>` you bring them back.

Case 2: Undoing a Rebase

Rebasing is a powerful feature of Git, allowing for cleaner, linear commit histories. However, it is also a common scenario where things can go wrong.

Perhaps you have initiated a rebase and realized that you have made a mistake.

With `git reflog`, you can easily undo the rebase, returning to your previous state before the rebase began, ensuring that your commit history stays in order, and your work is safe.

Troubleshooting Common Issues

While `git reflog` is a powerful tool, it is not without its faults. Here are some common issues and their solutions:

Issue: Reflog Not Showing Lost Commits

In some cases, you might find that `git reflog` is not showing the lost commits you are looking for. This could be due to a variety of reasons, including garbage collection in Git, which can prune orphaned commits.

Solution: Ensure that you use `git reflog` as soon as possible after realizing you have lost commits. The quicker you act, the higher the chances of recovering your lost work.

Issue: Ambiguous Reference in Git Reflog

Sometimes, when trying to recover lost commits, you might encounter an ambiguous reference error.

Solution: Ensure that you are using the correct reference from the `git reflog` output. Pay attention to the unique identifiers to avoid ambiguity.

`git reflog` is like strong support for developers dealing with the challenges of code versioning. It is a tool that, when you understand it well, gives you peace of mind and a feeling of safety. You know your work is secure, even if there are mistakes along the way.

Submodules in Git

Submodules in Git play a critical role when you are managing a larger project that depends on external code or libraries. Think of it like this – you have a big puzzle, and one of the pieces is another, smaller puzzle. This smaller puzzle is your submodule. It is a separate project but an essential part of your main project.

Let us dive deep into the concept of submodules, explore how they work, and understand how to use them effectively in our projects.

Purpose of Using Submodules

The beauty of submodules lies in their ability to let you include other Git repositories as a subdirectory of your project. This ensures that you are always working with the correct version of the external code. Consider a scenario where you are developing a web application that relies on a third-party library. If the library gets an update, your project might not be compatible with the new version right away. By using a submodule, you can control exactly which version of the third-party library your project uses, ensuring stability and consistency across all development environments.

Moreover, when others clone your project, Git makes it easy for them to also fetch the external dependencies (the submodules), ensuring that they have all the necessary components to run and work on the project right away. This removes the often-encountered problem of "**It works on my machine**," ensuring a smooth setup and onboarding process for new developers or collaborators.

Setting Up and Cloning Submodules

Now, let us understand the different steps for setting up a submodule.

1. **Adding a Submodule to Your Project**

Start by navigating to the root directory of your Git project where you wish to add a submodule.

Use the command to add a submodule:

```
git submodule add <repository-url> <path>
```

Replace `<repository-url>` with the URL of the repository you want to include as a submodule and `<path>` with the directory path where you want the submodule to reside within your project.

2. **Cloning a Project with Submodules**

When you clone a repository that contains submodules, the submodule directories are initially empty. To initialize and update them, run:

```
git clone --recursive <repository-url>
```

If you have already cloned the main project without the `--recursive` option, you can initialize and update submodules by running:

```
git submodule init
git submodule update
```

3. **Making Changes Within a Submodule**

Navigate into the submodule directory:

```
cd <path-to-submodule>
```

Make your changes, commit them, and push as you would with a regular Git repository:

```
git add .
git commit -m "Update submodule"
git push
```

After pushing the changes, navigate back to your main project directory. Git will detect changes in the submodule and will show the submodule directory as modified.

Commit this change to record the new commit ID of the submodule:

```
git add <path-to-submodule>
git commit -m "Update submodule to latest commit"
git push
```

4. **Pulling Updates for Submodules**

To pull updates for all submodules, you can use:

```
git submodule update --remote
```

This command fetches the latest changes from the remote repositories of each submodule and updates your local submodule directories to point to the most recent commits.

5. **Removing a Submodule**

If you need to remove a submodule from your project, you must:

- Delete the relevant section from the `.gitmodules` file.
- Delete the relevant section from `.git/config`.
- Run `git rm --cached <path-to-submodule>` to remove the submodule from the index.
- Commit your changes.
- Delete the unused submodule files from your working directory.

By following these steps, you can effectively manage external code dependencies in your projects, ensuring that everyone on the team works with the correct versions of each submodule, enhancing collaboration and reducing "*It works on my machine*" problems.

Working with Submodules

After you have added a submodule, any changes that you make inside the submodule directory are treated as changes to the submodule itself and should be committed and pushed from within the submodule directory. This is an important concept to grasp; the main project only tracks the submodule's commit ID, not its content. So, if you make changes to the submodule and commit them to the main project without pushing the changes in the submodule, other collaborators will not be able to get the latest changes in the submodule.

Furthermore, if a collaborator has made changes and pushed them to the submodule repository, you will need to pull these changes manually by navigating into the submodule directory, pulling the changes, and then going back to your main project and committing the change to the submodule's commit ID. It ensures that everyone working on the project is on the same page regarding the versions of submodules being used.

Real-Time Example: Managing a Plugin System

Let us talk about a real-time example to put things into perspective. Imagine you are working on a **content management system** (**CMS**), and this CMS has a plugin system. Each plugin is developed as a separate project and has its own Git repository. By using submodules, you can include these plugins in your CMS as subdirectories.

Now, consider that one of the plugins gets an update. Without submodules, you might need to download the updated version manually, ensure it is placed in the correct directory, and then make sure every developer on your team does the same. With submodules, you can simply pull the latest changes of the submodule, test it in your local environment to ensure compatibility, and then push the change of the submodule's commit ID to your main project. Every other developer can then fetch these changes, and they will all be working with the same, updated version of the plugin.

Now, let us see the steps to include a plugin as a submodule in your CMS:

1. **Add the Plugin as a Submodule:**

```
git submodule add https://example.com/plugin-repo.git plugins/plugin-name
```

2. **Clone the CMS Repository:**

```
git clone --recursive https://example.com/your-cms-repo.git
```

3. **Update a Plugin:**

Navigate to the plugin directory:

```
cd plugins/plugin-name
```

4. **Pull the latest changes and push the update to the main project:**

```
git pull
cd ../..
git add plugins/plugin-name
git commit -m "Update plugin-name to latest version"
git push
```

That is all. Now, you see with the help of the git submodule it becomes easy to manage multiple plugins without manual efforts.

Tips for Managing Submodules Effectively

Working with submodules can be a bit tricky, especially when you are new to it. Here are some tips to help you manage submodules effectively:

Stay Organized

Always keep your submodules in a specific directory within your project. This makes it easy to identify them and work with them.

Document the Setup

Ensure that you have clear documentation on how to clone and initialize the submodules for new developers or collaborators.

Regular Updates

Keep your submodules up to date and ensure that you regularly pull the latest changes and test them in your environment.

Submodules in Git provide a robust way of managing external dependencies, ensuring consistency and stability across all development environments. By mastering submodules, you equip yourself with a tool that can significantly streamline the management of external code and libraries in your projects, it helps everyone work together better and makes the development process smoother and more efficient.

Understanding Git Worktree

Imagine you are in the middle of implementing a new feature on a branch, and suddenly there is a critical bug that needs immediate attention on another branch. Normally, you would have to commit or stash your current changes, switch to the bugfix branch, make the necessary fixes, and then switch back to your feature branch. This can be quite cumbersome and breaks the flow of work. This is where `Git worktree` shines.

`Git worktree` allows you to create multiple working directories attached to the same Git repository, each pointing to a different branch. So instead of stashing and switching, you can simply move to a different directory and continue your work seamlessly. This feature is very useful for managing large codebases and working on complex projects where context switching is common.

Real-Time Example: Managing Feature Development and Bug Fixes

Let us consider a real-life scenario to better understand the practical implications of this feature. Assume you are working on a large web application, and you are in the midst of developing a new feature on a branch named `new-feature`.

Suddenly, a high-priority bug is reported in the live version of the application. The bug needs to be fixed on the `master` branch and deployed as soon as possible.

With `Git worktree`, you can navigate to your repository's directory in your Terminal or command prompt and run the following commands:

```
git worktree add ../bugfix master
```

Now, the output command of `git worktree add ../bugfix master` is shown in *Figure* 8.10:

```
(venv) PravinMishra@Pravin-MacBook-Pro ~ git worktree add ../bugfix master
Preparing worktree (checking out 'master')
HEAD is now at 8d47831 Update index.html
```

Figure 8.10**: Output of the Command **worktree add ../bugfix master

Now move to the `/bugfix`:

```
cd ../bugfix
```

Now, the output command of `cd ../bugfix` is shown in *Figure* 8.11:

```
(venv) PravinMishra@Pravin-MacBook-Pro ~ cd ../bugfix
(venv) PravinMishra@Pravin-MacBook-Pro ~ git branch
  feature-A
  feature-B
  main
* master
+ new-feature
```

Figure 8.11*: Output of the command " cd ../bugfix "*

This will create a new working directory named `bugfix` that is linked to the `master` branch. You can now fix the bug, commit the changes, and deploy the fix without having to disrupt your work on the `new-feature` branch. Once the fix is deployed, you can simply go back to your `new-feature` directory and continue your work. The context switch was handled smoothly without any need to stash changes or switch branches within a single working directory.

Now, let us delve deeper into understanding how `Git worktree` enhances our workflow. When you create a new worktree, Git creates a new directory on your file system, but it does not duplicate the entire repository. Instead, it creates a symbolic link to the original repository's objects, making it incredibly space-efficient.

Benefits of Using Git Worktree

Here are some benefits of using Git worktree:

Context Preservation

Each worktree has its own HEAD, staging area, and working directory, preserving the context of each line of work. This means you can have a worktree for feature development, another for bug fixes, and another for experimentation, each in its own context, ready to be picked up where you left off.

Parallel Work

You can work on multiple branches in parallel without disrupting the flow of work on any of them. This is particularly useful when you need to address critical issues on the production branch while continuing to work on features or improvements on other branches.

Code Review and Testing

You can have a dedicated worktree for code review or testing purposes, where you can switch between branches without affecting your main line of work. This creates a smoother code review process and ensures that testing does not stop the ongoing development.

Continuous Integration and Deployment

In a continuous integration and deployment (CI/CD) environment, you can have a worktree dedicated to preparing releases. This worktree can be used to perform final checks, run automated tests, and ensure everything is in order before deployment, all while development continues in other worktrees.

Best Practices and Tips for Using Git Worktree

Let us talk about the advantages of using Git Worktree. It is a feature that brings some useful benefits to your workflow.

Organizing Worktrees

It is a good practice to create a separate directory to house all your worktrees. This helps in keeping your workspace organized and makes it easier to navigate between different lines of work.

Naming Worktrees

Give your worktrees descriptive names that clearly indicate the purpose or branch they are associated with. This reduces confusion and helps you quickly identify the right worktree for the task at hand.

Cleaning Up

Remember to delete worktrees that are no longer needed. You can do this using the `git worktree remove` command, followed by the name of the worktree. This ensures your workspace stays clean and manageable.

Now, the output command of `git worktree remove` is shown in *Figure* 8.12:

```
(venv) PravinMishra@Pravin-MacBook-Pro ~ git worktree remove -f bugfix
```

***Figure 8.12**: Output of the command " git worktree remove "*

Avoiding Pitfalls

Be cautious not to delete the worktree directory using file system commands without properly removing it using Git commands, as this can lead to inconsistencies in the worktree configuration.

Troubleshooting Common Issues

While `Git worktree` is a great feature, it is not without its quirks. Following are some common issues that users might face, along with their solutions:

Detached HEAD State

When you add a new worktree, it might sometimes be in a detached `HEAD` state. This means any commits you make will not be on any branch. To resolve this, simply create a new branch or checkout an existing branch in the worktree.

Corrupted Worktrees

In some cases, worktrees can become corrupted, especially if they are not properly removed. If you encounter any inconsistencies or errors, you can use the `git worktree repair` command to fix the issue.

Pruning Stale Worktrees

Over time, you might accumulate stale worktrees that are no longer in use. You can clean these up using the `git worktree prune` command, which removes worktree administrative files that belong to worktrees that are no longer present on disk.

Now, the output command of `git worktree prune` is shown in *Figure* 8.13:

```
(venv) PravinMishra@Pravin-MacBook-Pro ~ git worktree list
/Users/sonali/the_cloudadvisory  4373370 [new-feature]
/Users/sonali/bugfix1            8d47831 [bugfix1] prunable
/Users/sonali/bugfix2            8d47831 [bugfix2]
(venv) PravinMishra@Pravin-MacBook-Pro ~ git worktree prune
(venv) PravinMishra@Pravin-MacBook-Pro ~ git worktree list
/Users/sonali/the_cloudadvisory  4373370 [new-feature]
/Users/sonali/bugfix2            8d47831 [bugfix2]
```

Figure 8.13: *Output of the command "**git worktree prune**"*

Learning about `Git worktree` helps you manage different tasks better, making it easier to switch between them and improving how much work you can do. It is a great feature in Git, showing how flexible and strong Git can be. It solves a problem that many developers face. So, start using it smartly and see how it changes how you work, making you a better and faster developer.

Advanced Configuration and Aliases

In this section, we will explore advanced Git configuration and the art of using aliases, all aimed at making your Git experience smoother, more efficient, and tailored to your workflow.

Understanding the Basics of Git Configuration

Before diving deep into advanced configurations, it is important to know the basic levels at which Git can be configured. Git configuration settings can be applied at three levels:

System level

These are the settings applied across the system, affecting all users on a machine. The configuration file for this level is usually found in `/etc/gitconfig`.

Global level

These settings are specific to your user profile on your computer, and they are stored in `~/.gitconfig` or `~/.config/git/config`.

Local Level

These settings are specific to a single repository, stored in `.git/config` inside the repository.

Understanding these levels is key to applying configurations effectively and ensuring that the settings behave as expected.

Streamlining Your Workflow with Aliases

One of the most powerful features in Git when it comes to customization is the ability to create aliases. Aliases in Git allow you to create shortcuts for commands, which can significantly speed up your workflow and reduce the time spent typing repetitive commands. Let us go through some practical examples to illustrate this.

Basic Aliases for Common Commands

If you find yourself typing `git status` frequently, you might create an alias like `st` to shorten the command:

```
git config --global alias.st status
```

Now, typing `git st` will execute `git status`. Simple changes like these can lead to significant time savings over the long run.

Complex Aliases for Streamlining Workflows

Aliases can also be used for more complex command sequences. For example, if you want to see a pretty log format with each commit on a single line, you can create an alias like this:

```
git config --global alias.lg "log --graph --pretty=format:'%C(auto)%h %s %d %C(black)%C(bold)%cr%C(reset)' --abbrev-commit"
```

Now, the output command of `git config --global alias.lg "log --graph --pretty=format:'%C(auto)%h %s %d %C(black)%C(bold)%cr%C(reset)' --abbrev-commit"` is shown in *Figure 8.14*:

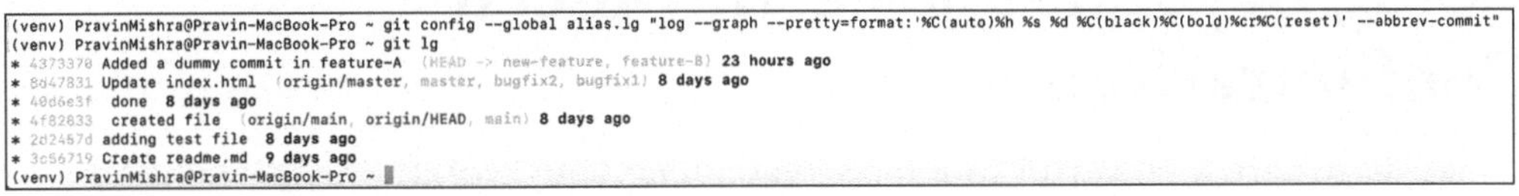

Figure 8.14: *Output of the command "git config"*

With this alias, typing `git lg` will display a beautifully formatted and color-coded Git log.

Using Aliases to Simplify Complex Commands

There are Git commands that, due to their complexity and the number of options available, can become quite lengthy and hard to remember. One such command is the interactive rebase command, which is used for rewriting commit history. Instead of typing out the full command each time, you can create an alias:

```
git config --global alias.ri "rebase -i"
```

Now, you can initiate an interactive rebase with a simpler `git ri`.

Aliases for Troubleshooting and Diagnostics

When you encounter issues in your repository, having quick access to diagnostic commands can be a lifesaver. Here is an example alias that shows you the size of your repository, which can be helpful in identifying performance issues:

```
git config --global alias.repo-size "count-objects -vH"
```

Now, the output command of "`git config --global alias.repo-size "count-objects -vH"` " is shown in *Figure 8.15*:

```
(venv) PravinMishra@Pravin-MacBook-Pro ~ git config --global alias.repo-size "count-objects -vH"

(venv) PravinMishra@Pravin-MacBook-Pro ~ git repo-size
count: 39
size: 156.00 KiB
in-pack: 3
packs: 1
size-pack: 1.82 KiB
prune-packable: 0
garbage: 0
size-garbage: 0 bytes
```

Figure 8.15: *Output of the command "git config --global alias.repo-size "count-objects -vH" "*

Executing `git repo-size` will now give you a detailed breakdown of your repository's size, helping you pinpoint issues and optimize storage.

Going Beyond Aliases: Advanced Configurations

While aliases are a powerful tool for streamlining your workflow, Git's configuration capabilities go far beyond just creating shortcuts. Let us explore some of the advanced configuration options available.

Fine-Tuning Your Diff Settings

When you are working with a team or on a project that involves frequent changes, having a clear and readable diff output is crucial. You can configure Git to use specific tools and settings for generating diffs, making the output more helpful. For example:

```
git config --global diff.renames copies
```

This setting tells Git to detect and show renamed and copied files in the diff output, providing a clearer picture of the changes made.

Customizing Commit Messages

Commit messages are a critical part of any project's history, providing context and rationale for changes. You can configure Git to launch a specific editor for writing commit messages, ensuring consistency and encouraging best practices. Here is how you can set Vim as your commit message editor:

```
git config --global core.editor "vim"
```

Now, every time you commit, Git will open Vim for you to write your commit message.

Enhancing Security with Signed Commits

In environments where security and verification are important, signing commits with GPG keys ensures that the changes come from a trusted source. You can configure Git to sign your commits by default:

```
git config --global commit.gpgSign true
```

With this configuration, every commit you make will be signed, providing an additional layer of security and verification to your workflow.

Sharing Configurations across Teams and Projects

In collaborative environments, ensuring that every member of the team has a consistent Git configuration can prevent issues and streamline workflows. You can create a shared Git configuration file and distribute it among your team members, encouraging best practices and consistency across the board.

Tailoring Git to your specific needs through advanced configuration and aliases is not just about saving time; it is about creating a more intuitive, efficient, and enjoyable development experience. By understanding the depths of what Git offers in terms of customization, you are equipping yourself with the tools to navigate the complexities of software development with ease and precision.

Whether it is creating simple aliases to reduce repetitive typing, fine-tuning your **diff settings** for clearer change tracking, or enforcing security practices with signed commits, the power to change Git into your ideal tool is at your fingertips. And as you continue to grow and evolve in your development journey, these skills and configurations will serve as a solid foundation, propelling you toward mastery of your craft.

Now that we have laid the foundation and equipped you with practical knowledge on advanced Git configurations and aliases, the journey towards a more streamlined and personalized Git experience has just begun. As you apply these techniques and continue to explore the vast capabilities of Git, remember that the tool is as powerful as your understanding and mastery of it.

Understanding Git Hooks

At its core, `Git hooks` are simply scripts that Git can execute before or after certain important actions, such as committing changes, pushing commits to a remote repository, or receiving changes from others. These scripts are stored in the hooks directory within your Git repository's `.git` directory, and they offer a way to trigger custom scripts at crucial points in your Git workflow.

Now, the output command of `Git hooks` is shown in *Figure 8.16*:

```
(venv) PravinMishra@Pravin-MacBook-Pro ~ cd .git
(venv) PravinMishra@Pravin-MacBook-Pro ~ ls
AUTO_MERGE      FETCH_HEAD    ORIG_HEAD    description    index    logs       objects        refs
COMMIT_EDITMSG  HEAD          config       hooks          info     modules    packed-refs    worktrees
(venv) PravinMishra@Pravin-MacBook-Pro ~ cd hooks
```

***Figure 8.16**: Output of the command "git hooks"*

Enforcing Coding Standards

One of the most common use cases for Git hooks is enforcing coding standards and styles across a project. Imagine you are leading a team of developers working on a large-scale software application. Consistency in coding style is paramount, as it ensures readability and maintainability of the codebase. By implementing a pre-commit hook, you can automate the process of checking for coding style violations before a commit is even made. Tools such as ESLint for JavaScript or PEP 8 for Python can be integrated into your hook, halting the commit process if any violations are found. This ensures that all code committed to the repository adheres to the agreed-upon coding standards, reducing the need for style-related corrections in code reviews.

Automating Test Execution

Another important application of Git hooks is in the automation of test execution. Testing is crucial in making sure the software works well. With a pre-push hook, you can check if all unit tests pass before sending changes to the main storage. This helps a lot because it lowers the risk of adding mistakes to the code and makes sure that only good-quality code is shared with the team or put into use.

Facilitating Continuous Integration

Git hooks also play a crucial role in facilitating **Continuous Integration** (**CI**) practices. In a typical CI workflow, code changes are continuously integrated into the project, and automated tests are run to validate these changes. By utilizing the post-receive hook on the remote repository, you can trigger a CI server to automatically fetch the latest changes and execute the test suite, ensuring that the integrated code is always in a releasable state.

Streamlining Code Reviews

In large teams, code reviews are a standard practice to ensure code quality and share knowledge among team members. A well-placed Git hook can streamline this process. For instance, a pre-push hook can be configured to ensure that all commits being pushed have passed code review, or that certain key files have been reviewed by specific individuals. This automated check ensures that no code skips the important review step, maintaining the integrity of the codebase.

Enforcing Branch Policies

Git hooks also offer a means to enforce branch policies, ensuring that developers follow the agreed-upon workflow. A common practice in many projects is to prevent direct commits to the main or master branch, ensuring that all changes go through a review process before being merged. A pre-commit or pre-push hook can be configured to check the current branch and block commits or pushes to the protected branches, guiding developers to create feature branches for their changes.

Managing Commit Messages

Well-formed commit messages are crucial for maintaining a readable and navigable Git history. They help you understand how the project has changed over time and find where specific changes came from. A `commit-msg` hook lets you make sure that commit messages follow a certain format, keeping things consistent throughout the project. It could be making sure messages start with a ticket number, follow a specific template, or are at least a certain length. This hook helps keep the project's Git history tidy and full of useful information.

Automating Release Tasks

When it comes to releasing a new version of your software, there are often a series of tasks that need to be completed, such as updating version numbers, generating changelogs, or creating tags. A `post-commit` or `post-merge` hook can help do these tasks automatically. This makes it easier during a release, and it makes sure no steps get forgotten.

Enhancing Collaboration

In collaborative projects, keeping all team members on the same page is important. A post-merge hook can be used to notify team members when new changes are merged, ensuring that everyone is aware of the latest developments. This could be in the form of an email notification, a message in a team chat, or any other means of communication that suits your team's workflow.

Backing Up Your Work

Data loss is a concern in any field of work, and software development is no exception. A post-commit hook can be used to create automatic backups of your repository each time a commit is made, ensuring that you have a recent version of your work saved in case of any mishaps.

Mastering the use of Git hooks is a path to making your development process smoother, more organized, and efficient. They help you automate tasks, set standards, and improve teamwork, making sure your project runs well and keeps a high level of quality. When you have the right hooks in action, your Git repository becomes a strong tool. It does not just track changes but actively contributes to the success and quality of your project. As we continue with Git, embracing the power of hooks is a move toward becoming a more skilled, efficient, and collaborative developer.

Large File Storage with Git LFS

Traditional Git repositories are designed to handle source code efficiently, but when it comes to large binary files like images, videos, or libraries, they can quickly become difficult. This is where **Git LFS** (Large File Storage) comes into play.

Git LFS is a Git extension that aims to make handling large files more efficient. It works by storing these large files on a separate server, while keeping a reference to the file in the Git repository. This means that your repository stays light, while still maintaining access to the large files when needed. In this section, we will explore how to use Git LFS, its benefits, and best practices for managing large binary files in your projects.

Getting Started with Git LFS

To start using Git LFS, you first need to install it on your system. The installation process is straightforward and varies depending on your operating system. Once installed, you need to configure Git LFS for your repository. This involves running a few simple commands in your terminal or command prompt to initialize Git LFS and specify the types of files you want to store in LFS.

Now, the output command of `brew install git-lfs` is shown in *Figure* 8.17:

```
(venv) PravinMishra@Pravin-MacBook-Pro ~ brew install git-lfs
Running `brew update --auto-update`...
```

***Figure* 8.17**: *Output of the command "brew install git-lfs"*

Now, the output command of `"git lfs install"` is shown in *Figure* 8.18:

```
(venv) PravinMishra@Pravin-MacBook-Pro ~ git lfs install
Updated Git hooks.
Git LFS initialized.
```

***Figure* 8.18**: *Output of the command git lfs install*

Adding Large Files to Git LFS

After configuration, adding large files to Git LFS is as simple as adding any other file to a Git repository. You use the `git add` command followed by a commit. However, instead of the large file being stored directly in the repository, a pointer file is stored in its place, and the actual file is stored on the LFS server. This keeps your repository size small and manageable, while still allowing you access to the large files when needed.

Benefits of Using Git LFS

Let us know about some benefits of using Git LFS:

Improved Performance

One of the most significant benefits of using Git LFS is the improved performance. Cloning and pulling from a repository with large files can be a time-consuming process when those files are stored directly in the repository. With Git LFS, these operations are much faster because you are only downloading the pointer files, not the large files themselves.

Version Control for Large Files

Git LFS also provides version control for large files, something that can be challenging to achieve with traditional methods. Every time you make a change to a large file and commit that change, Git LFS ensures that all versions of the file are accessible, allowing you to switch between versions just as you would with source code.

Collaboration and Consistency

When working on a team, ensuring that everyone has access to the same version of a large file is crucial. Git LFS ensures that all team members have access to the same files, preventing inconsistencies and streamlining the collaboration process.

Real-World Examples and Use Cases

Let us talk about the advantages of using Git LFS, a tool that brings some really helpful benefits to the table. These benefits make your experience with managing files smoother and more efficient. Let us dive into the details.

Game Development

In game development, large binary files such as textures, models, and sounds are commonplace. Managing these files can be a nightmare without the right tools. With Git LFS, game developers can store these large files efficiently, ensuring that the repository remains fast and responsive, while still maintaining version control and easy access to all assets.

Machine Learning

Machine learning projects often involve large datasets and model files. Git LFS provides a way to manage these files efficiently, ensuring that datasets and models are versioned and accessible, without bogging down the repository.

Media Production

In media production, whether it is video, audio, or graphics, large files are common. Git

LFS helps people handling media to handle these files well. It makes sure all versions of a media file are easy to get to, and the storage place stays fast and responsive.

Best Practices for Using Git LFS

Here are some tips to follow when using Git LFS.

Regularly Prune LFS Objects

As time goes on, the LFS server can gather many objects, using up a lot of storage space. It is important to regularly remove LFS objects that are no longer needed. This helps free up space and keeps the server working well.

Use Git LFS in Conjunction with a Suitable Hosting Service

To make the most of Git LFS, it is important to use it with a good hosting service that supports Git LFS. There are many options, like GitHub, GitLab, and Bitbucket. All of them give strong support for Git LFS.

Be Mindful of Bandwidth and Storage Quotas

When using Git LFS, be mindful of bandwidth and storage quotas imposed by the hosting service. Going beyond these limits might cost more money or make things slower.

Troubleshooting Common Issues

Let us talk about common issues you might face with Git LFS and how to troubleshoot them. These issues can include missing LFS objects and slow performance. Git LFS is a handy tool for handling large binary files in Git repositories, making tasks faster and collaboration smoother. Despite some challenges, knowing how to troubleshoot and follow best practices ensures that Git LFS works well for you, keeping your repository light and efficient. Whether you are into game development, machine learning, or media creation, Git LFS can significantly improve how you handle big files in your projects. Let us dive into how to address these common problems and make the most out of Git LFS.

Missing LFS Objects

A common problem with Git LFS is not having all the LFS objects. This happens when someone copies a repository but does not have Git LFS installed, or when the LFS objects are not sent correctly to the LFS server. To fix this, make sure Git LFS is installed and that all LFS objects are sent right to the LFS server.

Slow Performance

Slow performance when using Git LFS can happen because of different things, like problems with your internet, issues with the server, or having lots of LFS objects. To fix this, check your internet connection, make sure the LFS server is doing well, and think about getting rid of unnecessary LFS objects.

Handling big binary files in Git repositories can be hard, but with Git LFS, it becomes easier. Git LFS makes things faster, lets you control versions of big files, and makes working together smoother. It is a must-have tool for any project dealing with large binary files.

By following the best ways of doing things and fixing common problems, you can make sure Git LFS works really well for you. This keeps your repository light and quick while still giving you what you need from the big files. Whether you are into game development, machine learning, or making media, Git LFS is a tool that can change how you deal with big files, making your work better and more efficient. So, use the power of Git LFS and improve your projects.

Conclusion

Throughout this chapter, we have gone through the details of advanced Git features, digging deep into each topic to make sure you understand and can use the tools well. From comparing rebase and merge to getting good at interactive rebasing, cherry-picking, and using bisect to find bugs precisely, we have covered a lot of advanced Git stuff that is important for any experienced developer.

Remember, learning Git is an ongoing process. The more you practice and understand these advanced techniques, the better you will get. Keep practicing, exploring, and do not avoid challenges. With the foundation that we have built in this chapter, you are ready to handle Git's complexities with confidence and skill.

As we move to the next chapter, we are about to discover the exciting world of GitOps. In the next chapter, we will explore different tools and practices that show the GitOps idea. This will give you a full understanding and the skills to use this new approach in your own projects. So, get ready to dive into GitOps, where the best practices of software development meet operational excellence.

CHAPTER 9
GitOps: The Future of Operations

Introduction

Over the years, the world of IT has seen many changes, and one of the most notable shifts is the rise of GitOps. In this chapter, we will explore GitOps in a simple and practical way, understanding real-world examples to help you grasp this concept easily. Think of this chapter as your guide to understanding GitOps – a powerful combination of Git and DevOps operational patterns that is shaping the future of how we handle operations.

Structure

Here is what you can expect to learn in this chapter:

- Introduction to the GitOps Paradigm
- Principles of GitOps and Its Advantages
- How GitOps Revolutionizes CI/CD and Infrastructure as Code (IaC)
- Tools and Platforms Supporting GitOps
- Case Studies of GitOps in Action
- GitOps Security Considerations
- Getting Started with GitOps
- Monitoring and Observability in GitOps
- GitOps for Multi-Cloud and Hybrid Environments
- GitOps Policy Management and Compliance
- GitOps Workflow Optimization
- Integration with Existing Tools and Systems
- Future Trends and Developments in GitOps

By the end of this chapter, you will not only understand the theoretical concept of GitOps but also acquire the practical skills to implement and optimize it within your operations.

Introduction to the GitOps

GitOps is a method that builds on DevOps practices, such as continuous integration and continuous delivery (CI/CD). It applies the principles of version control to automate the management of infrastructure and software deployment. It allows developers to define the desired state of their infrastructure in Git repositories and leverage git set up to automate and manage operational processes effectively.

So GitOps is centered around tools. GitOps extends the use of Git from managing application source code to include application configurations, infrastructure, and operational procedures.

As you notice, you can store all components of a project's infrastructure, including code files, configuration files, and infrastructure as code files, in Git repositories. If there are any changes to applications and infrastructure code it will automatically synchronize with the live environment.

GitOps is versatile and can be applied across various infrastructures, proving especially valuable for software developers and platform engineers working with Kubernetes. It simplifies the deployment process for cloud-native applications by ensuring that the cloud infrastructure can be quickly reproduced based on the current state of a Git repository.

GitOps is Not a Replacement for DevOps

It is important to understand that GitOps is not a replacement for DevOps or an evolution like "*DevOps 2.0*". Rather, it introduces a set of practices focused on deployment while DevOps focus on a broader philosophy aimed at improving collaboration across development and operations teams. The shared principles between GitOps and DevOps facilitate an easier adoption of GitOps workflows, enhancing existing DevOps techniques.

From Version Control to Operations: A Natural Progression

The evolution from version control to operations through GitOps represents a logical advancement in how we approach software development and infrastructure management.

Traditionally, version control systems like Git have been necessary for tracking changes in software development, offering teams the ability to collaborate more effectively on coding projects. GitOps takes this foundational practice a step further, applying the disciplined, version-controlled approach that we have come to rely on for code to the entire operational infrastructure.

This progression acknowledges that the principles which make version control so effective for software development – such as traceability, collaboration, and rollback capabilities – also apply to infrastructure management. By treating **infrastructure as code (IaC)**, GitOps allows for the entire operational environment to be scripted, stored in Git repositories, and managed with the same as application source code. This means that changes to infrastructure undergo the same review processes, automated testing, and versioning that code changes do.

Furthermore, this approach seamlessly integrates with continuous integration and continuous delivery (CI/CD) pipelines, enabling automated deployment and management of infrastructure. With Git at the center, operations teams can now implement changes with confidence, knowing that every modification is tracked, reversible, and transparent. This shift not only enhances the reliability and stability of environments but also promotes a culture of collaboration between development and operations teams.

At its core, moving from version control to operations via GitOps is not just about adopting new tools or technologies. It is about applying a proven, effective methodology to a broader domain. By extending version control principles to operations, GitOps simplifies and streamlines the deployment process for cloud-native applications and infrastructure, ensuring quick, consistent, and secure environments.

As the divide between development and operations narrows, GitOps emerges as a natural progression in the evolution of DevOps practices. It underlines the integration of development and operational workflows, ensuring that infrastructure management benefits from the same level of precision and accountability as application development. This accommodation between development and operations highlights the way for more efficient, reliable, and collaborative IT environments, firmly establishing GitOps as a key component of modern software development and deployment strategies.

Now, let us understand GitOps with a real-time example.

Real-Time Applications: GitOps in Action

Imagine a software development team working on a cloud-native application that serves thousands of users daily. The application infrastructure, including servers, databases, and networking, is defined using IaC and stored in a Git repository. The team follows GitOps principles to manage this infrastructure, leading to a more streamlined and efficient deployment process. Here is how GitOps transforms their workflow.

Scenario

The team plans to roll out a new feature that requires updates to both the application code and the underlying infrastructure. This includes adding new services, updating database configurations, and adjusting network settings to accommodate increased traffic.

Step 1: Propose Changes Through Pull Requests

A developer creates a branch in the Git repository and makes necessary changes to the code and IaC configurations. This includes adding new Kubernetes deployment files and modifying existing Terraform scripts to make provision for additional resources.

They submit a pull request for the team to review the proposed changes.

Step 2: Automated Testing and Review

Upon submission, an automated CI pipeline kicks in, running tests to validate both the application changes and the infrastructure updates. This ensures that the new feature does not introduce errors or vulnerabilities.

Team members review the pull request, providing feedback or approval. This collaborative review process ensures a high level of code quality and adherence to best practices.

Step 3: Merge and Automatic Deployment

Once the pull request is approved, it is merged into the main branch. This merge triggers the Continuous Deployment (CD) pipeline.

The CD pipeline automatically applies the infrastructural changes to a staging environment using tools like Terraform and Kubernetes. The application is also deployed to this environment for final testing.

Step 4: Monitoring and Validation

The team monitors the staging deployment closely, checking system metrics and logs to ensure that everything operates as expected. Automated tests validate the new feature's functionality and performance under load.

After confirming the success of the deployment in the staging environment, the changes are promoted to production, where the CD pipeline replicates the process, updating the live environment automatically.

Step 5: Easy Rollback if Needed

In case it does not work as expected in the production environment, there are no issues. With every aspect of the infrastructure and application defined in code and version-controlled in Git, rolling back to the previous state is straightforward if any issues are discovered in production.

Outcome

The new feature is successfully deployed with minimal manual intervention. The entire process, from proposing changes to deploying in production, is faster, more secure, and more reliable.

That is the beauty of GitOps. GitOps empowers the team to maintain a high pace of innovation while ensuring stability and compliance with operational standards.

Now, let us understand the Principles of GitOps that you should follow.

Principles of GitOps

GitOps is not just a methodology, but a set of practices that can be followed through four key principles. Understanding these principles helps clarify why adopting GitOps can significantly benefit the development and operations teams alike.

- **Infrastructure as Code (IaC)**

  The foundation of GitOps lies in treating all aspects of infrastructure as code. By defining infrastructure using code, teams can leverage version control systems like Git to manage and track changes, ensuring consistency, transparency, and repeatability across environments. This principle facilitates automated testing and review processes, similar to those used for application development.

- **Immutable Infrastructure**

  GitOps advocates for creating infrastructure that, once deployed, is not modified directly. Instead, any necessary changes are made in the IaC, committed to the Git repository, and deployed as a new version of the infrastructure. This approach reduces inconsistencies between environments and enhances the reliability of deployments.

- **Continuous Deployment**

  Automated deployment pipelines are central to GitOps. By now you understand that every commit to the main branch triggers an automated deployment process, ensuring that the state of the infrastructure always matches the code in the repository. This automation reduces the potential for human error, speeds up deployment times, and supports a culture of continuous improvement.

- **Observability and Feedback Loops**

  GitOps emphasizes the importance of monitoring and logging to provide comprehensive observability of the system's state. This visibility is important for detecting issues early and informing the development process. Additionally, creating feedback loops through monitoring tools ensures that any deviation from the desired state is quickly identified and corrected.

  Great, now it is time to look at some of the advantages of using GitOps.

GitOps and Its Advantages

This could be a very long topic, and some points have been covered earlier. Now, let us understand five most important advantages of GitOps.

Enhanced Collaboration and Productivity

As you know, GitOps leverages tools and practices that development teams are already familiar with, lowering the barrier to entry for implementing infrastructure changes. This familiarity, combined with the pull request review process, enhances collaboration between development and operations teams, leading to higher productivity and faster innovation.

Improved Reliability and Stability

As a developer, when you define the entire infrastructure as code and automate deployments, GitOps minimizes the risk of human error and inconsistencies across environments, and this is a significant advantage.

The immutable infrastructure principle ensures that any changes are traceable and reversible, contributing to system stability and reliability.

Faster Recovery Times

The most important advantage for a production environment is the ability to quickly revert to a previous state of the infrastructure. It is only possible by combining with automated deployments that significantly reduce recovery time in the event of an issue. Teams can address problems swiftly without the need for manual intervention, minimizing downtime and improving service availability.

Simplified Compliance and Auditability

With all changes tracked in a version control system, GitOps provides a clear audit trail of who made what changes and when. This traceability simplifies compliance with regulatory requirements and makes it easier to conduct audits of infrastructure changes.

Streamlined Operations

By following all these practices, GitOps automates many of the manual tasks associated with deploying and managing infrastructure, allowing teams to focus on delivering value rather than on operational overheads. This streamlining of operations accelerates the delivery of new features and improvements, keeping pace with business demands.

So in summary, adopting GitOps can transform the way teams manage infrastructure and deploy applications, offering substantial advantages in terms of reliability, productivity, and compliance. Its principles align closely with modern development practices, making it an attractive option for teams looking to optimize their operations.

The following section explains some case studies that are drawn from my personal experience, and you might find them adaptable for use within your team or organization according to your specific requirements.

Case Studies of GitOps in Action

Now, let us explore some Case Studies of GitOps.

Change in a High-Stakes Deployment

- **The Challenge**

  A multinational financial institution, with a strict regulatory environment and a complex web of legacy systems, faced significant hurdles in its software deployment processes. The release cycles were slow and error-prone, causing delays and inefficiencies that rippled across operations.

- **The GitOps Solution**

  The organization implemented GitOps, restructuring their deployment pipeline around Git's robust version control. By using Git as the single source of truth, the deployment process became more transparent, auditable, and easier to manage.

- **The Outcome**

  Deployment times were slashed by over 70%, and errors in production dropped significantly. Moreover, the compliance teams could easily track changes and ensure adherence to regulatory requirements, thanks to the clear audit trail provided by Git.

Scaling Infrastructure with GitOps

- **The Challenge**

  An e-commerce company experiencing rapid growth was struggling to scale its infrastructure to meet increasing demand. Manual provisioning and configuration led to inconsistencies and outages during peak traffic periods.

- **The GitOps Solution**

  The team applied GitOps principles, managing their infrastructure as code. By automating provisioning and ensuring that all changes were committed to Git, they could scale resources up or down with the push of a button.

- **The Outcome**

  The e-commerce platform maintained high availability even during the biggest sales events, and the infrastructure team could focus on improving the system rather than fire-fighting problems.

Disaster Recovery with GitOps

- **The Challenge**

  A cloud services provider faced a critical disaster when a misconfiguration led to a significant service disruption. The pressure was on to restore services quickly and minimize downtime.

- **The GitOps Solution**

  With GitOps, they had a detailed record of every configuration change in their Git repository. This allowed them to quickly identify the faulty change and roll back to a previous, stable state without having to guess which configuration was to blame.

- **The Outcome**

  Service was restored in a fraction of the time it would have taken with traditional methods. The incident also demonstrated the need for tighter controls, which GitOps could facilitate through its pull request and review mechanisms.

Continuous Improvement with GitOps Feedback Loops

- **The Challenge**

  A software development agency was facing issues with keeping its development, staging, and production environments in sync. This led to the common "it works on my machine" syndrome, hindering reliable releases.

- **The GitOps Solution**

  By implementing a GitOps workflow, the team ensured that the same deployment process was used for every environment. This consistency helped in identifying environment-specific issues early in the development cycle.

- **The Outcome**

  The "*it works on my machine*" problem was virtually eliminated. Developers received immediate feedback if their changes did not work in the staging environment, which closely mirrored production.

GitOps in a Regulated Biotech Environment

- **The Challenge**

  A biotechnology company was required to maintain strict audit trails and reproducibility for their software used in clinical trials. The complexity of their systems made compliance a constant challenge.

- **The GitOps Solution**

  Adopting GitOps allowed them to leverage Git's version control for their entire operational stack, including the code, infrastructure, and even compliance policies as code.

- **The Outcome**

  Not only did they pass their compliance audits with flying colors, but they were also able to demonstrate the reproducibility of their computational environments, a significant win for both the IT and research teams.

  These case studies reveal the adaptability and strength of GitOps across different industries and challenges. They illustrate not just the successes but also how GitOps enables teams to quickly recover from setbacks. Through these real-world examples, we can see how GitOps is more than just a set of practices – it is a pathway to greater operational resilience and efficiency.

  Now, let us delve into a critical aspect of GitOps – Security. Understanding the security implications and best practices within GitOps is not only essential – it is a fundamental part of ensuring the integrity and reliability of your deployment workflow.

GitOps Security Considerations

As GitOps brings a lot of advantages, we must adapt security strategies to address the unique challenges and benefits that this method introduces. Here are strategies that have effectively protected pipelines while maintaining their speed and flexibility.

A Primer on GitOps and Security

To start, let us set the stage for what GitOps means in the context of security. Imagine GitOps as a highway. Your code and infrastructure are vehicles traveling toward their destination – deployment. Just as traffic laws and safety measures keep a road safe, certain protocols and tools ensure that your GitOps workflow is secure.

The Significance of 'Everything as Code'

In GitOps, everything is code – your infrastructure, your configurations, and even your policies. When you define everything as code, it can be tracked, reviewed, and managed in Git repositories. This is powerful because it gives you the ability to apply the same security to your operational changes as you do to your software code. Peer reviews, automated checks, and version control become your first line of defense against mistakes and malicious changes.

Immutable Infrastructure and Automated Pipelines

The concept of immutability is central to GitOps and a boon for security. By treating your environments as immutable, you rebuild from a known-good state with every change, rather than patching or updating on the fly. This drastically reduces the risk of a security misconfiguration going unnoticed.

Role-Based Access Control and Traceability

With GitOps, you implement **role-based access control** (**RBAC**) at the Git level. This means individuals have only the access necessary for their role, limiting the scope of what they can change. Every action is recorded in Git, which means every change is traceable back to the individual who made it, ensuring accountability.

Key Strategies for Securing Your GitOps Workflow

Now, let us dive into the specific strategies to keep GitOps workflows secure.

Strategy 1: Secure Your Code

The Git repository is the heart of your GitOps workflow. It is important to secure it like you would any valuable asset.

Protecting the Repository

- **Use Two-Factor Authentication (2FA)**: Every person who has access to your repository must have 2FA enabled. This adds an extra layer of defense against unauthorized access.

- **Limit Access**: Only necessary personnel should have write access to your repositories, especially those that drive your production environment.
- **Branch Protection Rules**: Implement rules that prevent direct pushes to critical branches and require pull requests for changes, ensuring that a review process is in place.

Managing Secrets

- **Avoid Storing Secrets in Git**: Sensitive data like passwords and tokens should never be stored plainly in your repositories. Use secret management tools that integrate with your CI/CD system.
- **Encryption**: If secrets must be in Git, ensure that they are encrypted and decrypted only within a secure environment.

Strategy 2: Review and Approve Changes

Incorporating a mandatory review process for all changes to your GitOps repositories is not just a good practice; it is a security essential.

Peer Review Processes

- **Mandatory Peer Reviews**: All changes should be reviewed by at least one other team member before merging, providing a catch-net for potential security issues.
- **Automated Security Scanning**: Integrate tools that automatically scan pull requests for secrets or security vulnerabilities.

Policy as Code

- **Enforce Policies**: Use policy as code tools to enforce operational and security policies for your infrastructure. This means that any changes that do not comply with your security standards cannot be merged.

Strategy 3: Continuous Monitoring and Compliance

A secure GitOps process involves constant vigilance. Monitoring and compliance are continuous duties.

Audit Logs and Monitoring

- **Audit Trails**: Ensure that all actions in your repositories and CI/CD pipelines are logged, providing an audit trail for future reference in the event of an incident.
- **Anomaly Detection**: Set up monitoring to alert you of unusual activity, such as unexpected deployment at odd hours, which can be signs of a breach.

Compliance Checks

- **Automated Compliance Scanning**: Regularly scan your environment against compliance standards relevant to your organization.

Strategy 4: Disaster Recovery

Even with the best security, things can go wrong. That is why a disaster recovery plan is essential.

Backup and Restore Procedures

- **Regular Backups:** Regularly back up your Git repositories and ensure that your backup process includes your secret management systems.
- **Recovery Plans:** Have a clear plan for restoring from backups in the event of data corruption or loss.

Getting Started with GitOps

Now, let us understand the practicality of GitOps.

Building Your First GitOps Workflow

As you are just starting to build your first GitOps workflow, start simple. Choose a non-critical application and begin defining its desired state within your Git repository. Set up a simple pipeline that automates its deployment. Then, watch, learn, and iterate.

Let us walk through building your first GitOps workflow step by step. For this tutorial, we will use GitHub to host our repository and GitHub Actions as our automation tool to create a CI/CD pipeline. We will deploy a simple "Hello World" application.

Prerequisites

- A GitHub account.
- Basic understanding of Git commands.
- A simple application to deploy. If you do not have one, just create an `index.html` file with "Hello World" as its content.

Step 1: Create Your Repository

1. Log in to your GitHub account.
2. Click the **+** icon in the upper-right corner and select **`New repository`**.
3. Name your repository, for example, `hello-world-gitops`.

4. Choose **Public** or **Private** visibility as needed.
5. Click **Create repository**.

Step 2: Define the Desired State of Your Application

1. Clone the repository to your local machine:

```
git clone https://github.com/<your-username>/hello-world-gitops.git
```

2. Add your application files to this repository. For a simple start, create an index.html file with the following content:

```
<html>
<head>
    <title>Hello World</title>
</head>
<body>
    <h1>Hello World! Welcome to GitOps.</h1>
</body>
</html>
```

3. Push the changes to GitHub:

```
git add index.html
git commit -m "Add initial version of the application"
git push origin main
```

Step 3: Set Up a Simple Pipeline Using GitHub Actions

1. In your GitHub repository, navigate to the **Actions** tab (see *Figure 9.1*):

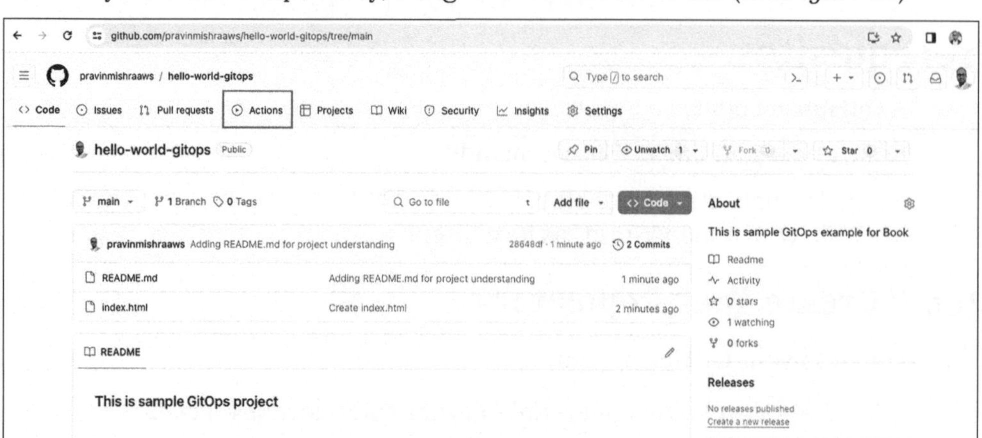

***Figure 9.1**: GitHub action*

2. Click on set up a workflow (see *Figure* 9.2) yourself.

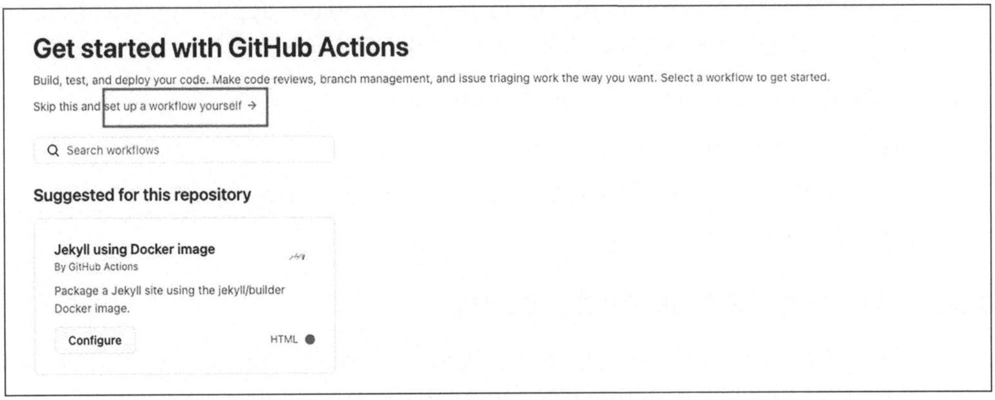

Figure 9.2*: Set up workflow*

3. GitHub will create a `.github/workflows/main.yml` file. Edit this file to define your CI/CD pipeline:

```
name: Deploy Hello World Application


on:
  push:
    branches:
      - main


jobs:
  build_and_deploy:
    runs-on: ubuntu-latest
    steps:
    - uses: actions/checkout@v2

    - name: Deploy to Server
      run: |
        # Add deployment commands here
        # For example, if deploying to an FTP server:
        # ftp -av --remove-source-files $FTP_SERVER $DEPLOY_PATH
```

4. Replace the placeholder comment with commands to deploy your application to your hosting environment. For instance, if you are deploying to a static site host, you might use scp or an FTP command to transfer files.
5. Commit the workflow file to your repository:

```
git add .github/workflows/main.yml
git commit -m "Create CI/CD pipeline for deployment"
git push origin main
```

Step 4: Watch, Learn, and Iterate

1. After pushing the changes, go to the Actions tab on your GitHub repository to watch the pipeline in action (see *Figure* 9.3):

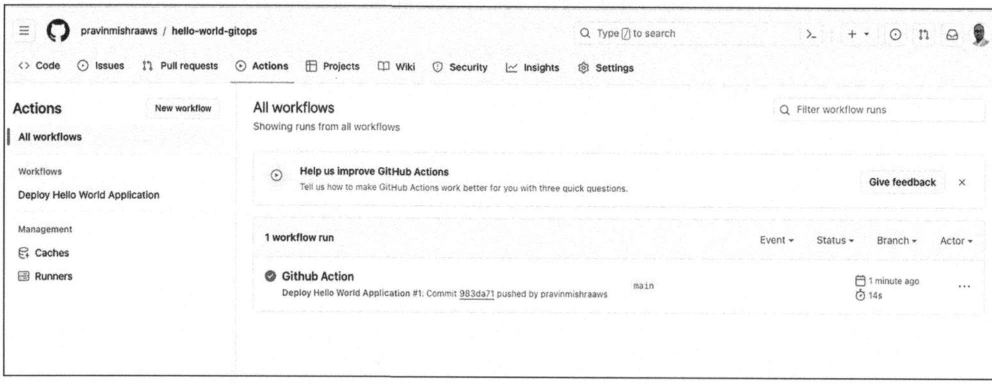

***Figure 9.3**: Pipeline in action*

2. If the pipeline fails, review the logs provided by GitHub Actions to troubleshoot and understand what went wrong.
3. Make the necessary adjustments to your pipeline configuration and your application, commit, and push again.

Step 5: Refining Your Workflow

1. As you become more comfortable with the basic deployment, start expanding your pipeline. Integrate additional steps like running tests or setting up notifications upon successful deployment.
2. Explore ways to make your deployment more robust, such as adding rollback capabilities in case of deployment failures.

This simple workflow is your stepping stone into the world of GitOps. By starting small, you have learned the basics of automating your deployment process using GitHub and

GitHub Actions. The key is to build upon this foundation, exploring more advanced features and tools as you grow.

Remember, GitOps is about incremental improvements and continuous learning. Keep iterating, and soon you will be deploying more complex applications with confidence.

This example was for application, now you must be thinking about how we build an infrastructure with GitOps.

Now, let us do this in the next example.

Building Modular Infrastructure as Code

One of the key strategies is the use of modular Infrastructure as Code (IaC). By breaking down your infrastructure into modular components, you make it easier to manage and update. It also enables different teams to work on separate pieces of the infrastructure without stepping on each other's toes, much like developing microservices for a large and complex application.

Let us build a Modular Infrastructure as Code (IaC) in AWS with GitOps!

In this example, we will guide you through setting up a modular IaC using AWS CloudFormation, managed through Git as a version control system in a GitOps workflow.

Prerequisites

1. An AWS account.
2. Basic understanding of AWS services like EC2, S3, VPC, and so on.
3. Familiarity with Git and GitHub.
4. Installed and configured AWS CLI on your local machine.
5. Installed Git on your local machine.

Step 1: Setting Up Your Project Repository

1. Create a New Repository:
    a. Log into GitHub.
    b. Create a new repository named `aws-modular-infra`.
2. Clone the Repository:
    a. On your local machine, run `git clone <repository-url>`

git clone https://github.com/pravinmishraaws/aws-modular-infra.git

b. Change into the cloned directory with `cd aws-modular-infra`

Step 2: Creating Your First Infrastructure Module

1. Define the Module:

   a. Inside the aws-modular-infra directory, create a new directory for the VPC module: `mkdir vpc`.

   b. Inside the vpc directory, create a new file named **vpc.yaml**.

2. Write the CloudFormation Template:

   a. Open **vpc.yaml** in your text editor.

   b. Define a basic VPC resource with CloudFormation syntax as below:

```
AWSTemplateFormatVersion: '2010-09-09'
Description: A basic VPC module
Resources:
  BasicVPC:
    Type: AWS::EC2::VPC
    Properties:
      CidrBlock: 10.0.0.0/16
      EnableDnsSupport: true
      EnableDnsHostnames: true
      Tags:
        - Key: Name
          Value: BasicVPC
```

3. Commit Your Module:

   a. Add the file to Git with

   ```
   git add vpc/vpc.yaml
   ```

   b. Commit the changes

   ```
   git commit -m "Add basic VPC module"
   ```

   c. Push the changes to GitHub with

   ```
   git push origin main
   ```

Step 3: Automating the Deployment with GitHub Actions

1. Create GitHub Actions Workflow:

    a. In the repository, create a directory `.github/workflows`

    b. Inside this directory, create a file `main.yml`

2. Set Up Your Workflow:

    a. Now define the workflow to deploy the CloudFormation template when changes are pushed to the main branch. Open the `main.yaml` file and write down the following code:

```
name: Deploy VPC Module


on:
  push:
    branches:
      - main


jobs:
  deploy:
    runs-on: ubuntu-latest
    steps:
      - name: Checkout
        uses: actions/checkout@v2

      - name: Configure AWS Credentials
        uses: aws-actions/configure-aws-credentials@v1
        with:
          aws-access-key-id: ${{ secrets.AWS_ACCESS_KEY_ID }}
          aws-secret-access-key: ${{ secrets.AWS_SECRET_
          ACCESS_KEY }}
          aws-region: us-west-2

      - name: Deploy CloudFormation Template
```

```
run: |
  aws cloudformation deploy \
    --template-file vpc/vpc.yaml \
    --stack-name basic-vpc-stack \
    --no-fail-on-empty-changeset \
    --capabilities CAPABILITY_IAM
```

Now, all set for GitHub action. But to create a VPC in an AWS account, we need Git to know our AWS credentials. So, the next step is to set up the AWS credentials.

3. Secure Your AWS Credentials:

   a. In your GitHub repository (remember, it's your Git repository, not your profile/account setting), go to **`Settings`** > **`Secrets`**.

   b. Add your `AWS_ACCESS_KEY_ID` and `AWS_SECRET_ACCESS_KEY` as secrets (see *Figure* 9.4):

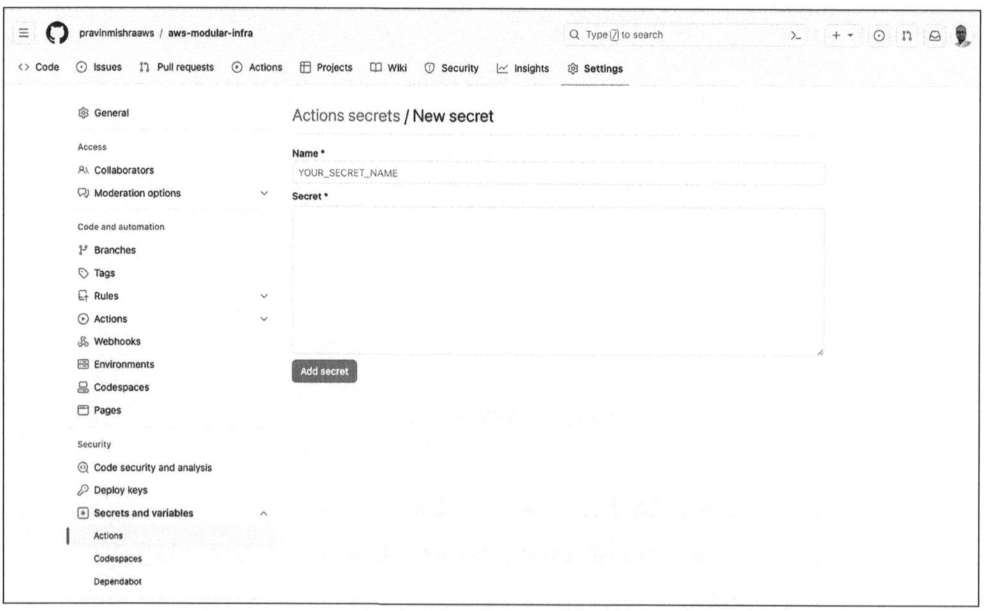

Figure 9.4: *AWS access keys*

4. Commit and Push Your Workflow:

   a. Add the workflow file to Git with

   ```
   git add .github/workflows/main.yml
   ```

b. Commit the changes with

```
git commit -m "Add deployment workflow"
```

c. Push the changes to GitHub with

```
git push origin main
```

Step 4: Monitoring and Iterating

1. Monitor the Workflow:

   a. Go to the **`Actions`** tab in your GitHub repository to see the workflow execution.

   b. Ensure that the CloudFormation stack is deployed successfully (see *Figure* 9.5)in AWS:

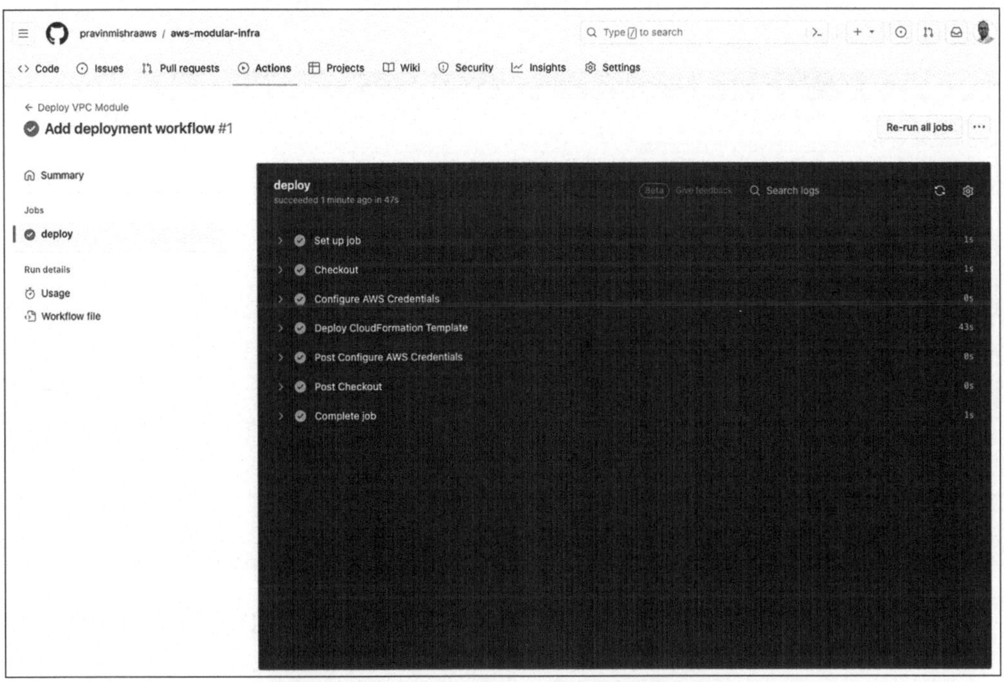

***Figure 9.5**: CloudFormation stack deployed*

2. See network in AWS:

   a. Now, go to your AWS account and ensure you are in Oregon (`us-west-2`) AWS region. Go to the `CloudFormation` dashboard, you will then see a CF stack with the name: `basic-vpc-stack` (*Figure* 9.6):

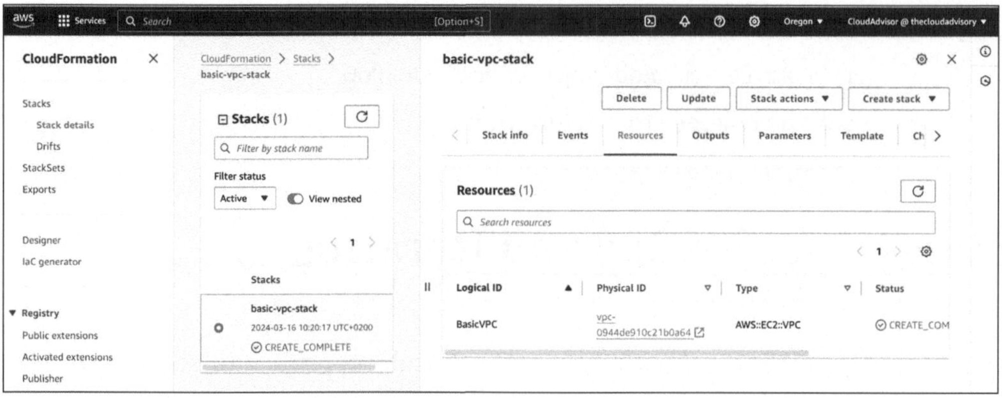

Figure 9.6: VPC stack

Now, click the **Resources** tab and then click the **Physical ID** of the VPC. This will take you to theAWS VPC dashboard, where you will see the AWS VPC (see Figure 9.7) created for you:

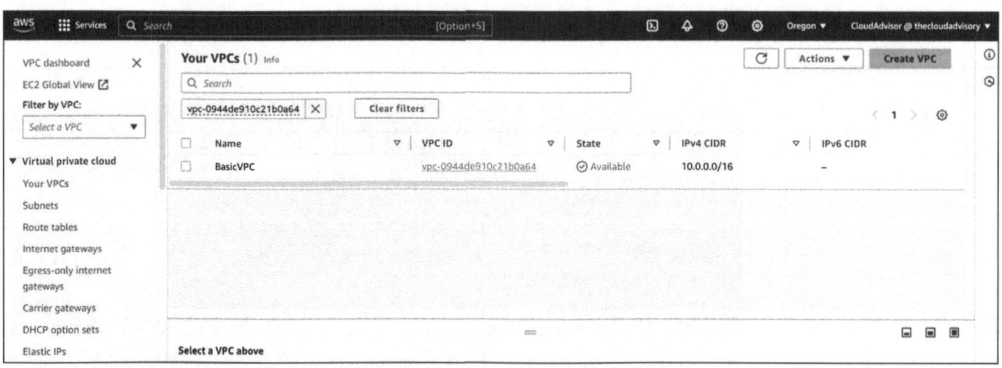

Figure 9.7: AWS VPC

3. Iterate and Expand:

    a. Create new modules for other AWS services following the same pattern.

    b. Use the **`CloudFormation Outputs`** section to export values from one module and import them into others.

You have now set up a basic modular IaC in AWS using CloudFormation, managed through a GitOps workflow with GitHub Actions. You can expand on this by adding more modules, creating dependencies between them, and further automating the deployment and update processes.

Automating for Consistency and Speed

In this previous section, we explored the practical application of GitOps principles to build a modular **Infrastructure as Code (IaC)** setup using AWS CloudFormation, managed through Git as the version control system. We have designed this example to guide you through the process of setting up a project repository, creating a basic **Virtual Private Cloud (VPC)** module, automating the deployment with GitHub Actions, and finally, monitoring the deployment in AWS.

The process began with establishing a new GitHub repository to house the project's IaC configurations. By creating a directory for a VPC module and defining the VPC with CloudFormation syntax, we demonstrated how infrastructure components can be modularized and version-controlled just like application code. This modular approach not only simplifies management but also enhances collaboration across teams, allowing for independent development on different infrastructure components without conflicts.

Automating the deployment process using GitHub Actions introduced a seamless integration between code changes and infrastructure updates. By specifying a workflow that triggers on push events to the main branch, we ensured that any changes to the VPC module would automatically deploy to AWS, making the infrastructure immediately reflective of the current state of the repository. This automation is central to GitOps, facilitating a consistent and reliable deployment process.

Securing AWS credentials in GitHub Secrets and leveraging them in the GitHub Actions workflow ensures the importance of security and best practices in managing access to cloud environments. This step is crucial for maintaining a secure and efficient CI/CD pipeline.

Monitoring the workflow execution and verifying the deployment in the AWS CloudFormation dashboard provided insights into the deployment process and the final outcome. This visibility is important for troubleshooting, auditing, and iterating on the infrastructure setup.

With the help of this example, you would have understood how GitOps can streamline and secure the process of deploying and managing cloud infrastructure using familiar tools like Git, GitHub Actions, and AWS CloudFormation.

Ongoing Evaluation and Iteration

Now, based on the previous example, you understand that you can build the entire AWS infrastructure for your application. Therefore, integrating GitOps is not a one-time event; it is a continuous process. Regular evaluations of how the integration is performing, and iterative improvements are key to a successful GitOps adoption. In the journey, we have set up quarterly reviews to assess the progress of GitOps integration and to make adjustments as needed.

Integrating GitOps into existing systems requires thoughtful planning, patience, and a willingness to adapt. It is a journey of transforming practices while honouring the past investments in technology and people. By following the aforementioned steps, you can weave GitOps into your organization's fabric, ensuring that you leverage the full spectrum of benefits that it offers.

Now, we cannot leave this amazing topic without talking about future trends and the development of GitOps. That is why the next topic is very important.

Future Trends and Developments in GitOps

As we have integrated GitOps into our workflows, we have seen remarkable improvements in deployment speed, stability, and scalability. Looking ahead, we envision a future where GitOps not only streamlines operations but also fundamentally transforms them.

Predicting the Path of Progress

In the near future, GitOps can be seen intersecting with **artificial intelligence** (**AI**) and **machine learning** (**ML**). These technologies could provide predictive analytics to foresee potential issues before they impact operations. Imagine a system where AI assists in automatically resolving merge conflicts or even suggests optimal deployment windows based on historical data.

GitOps and the Serverless Landscape

Serverless computing is another area ripe for GitOps innovation. As serverless architectures become more prevalent, GitOps principles could govern the deployment and management of these ephemeral resources, leading to more dynamic and responsive infrastructures.

Increased Focus on Security and Compliance

Security is an evergreen concern in IT, and GitOps will likely continue to evolve to address this. We might see more sophisticated security scanning tools integrated directly into GitOps workflows, automatically checking for vulnerabilities whenever a pull request is raised.

Cross-Platform GitOps Workflows

As cloud services grow more heterogeneous, there is a growing need for GitOps workflows that span across various platforms. It is predicted that we will see tools that manage multi-cloud and hybrid environments more seamlessly, allowing operations teams to maintain consistency across a diverse range of infrastructures.

The future of GitOps is not set in stone, but its trajectory is promising. As we continue to innovate and incorporate new technologies into our workflows, the potential for GitOps to further revolutionize IT operations is substantial. By staying attuned to these trends and remaining adaptable, we place ourselves in an excellent position to leverage the full power of GitOps in the years to come.

Conclusion

As we conclude this deep dive into GitOps, a way of doing things that seems like the future of operations, it is important to understand the big impact it has. In this chapter, we talked about GitOps, starting from the basics and going to why it is better than the usual CI/CD methods. We also looked at the tools that make it work and real-life examples that show how good it is. It helps things go smoothly, makes things secure, and encourages teamwork and transparency.

Next, we will talk about the best ways to use Git and GitHub in the upcoming chapter. We will build on what we talked about before and share tips to help you and your team get the most out of these powerful tools. Whether you are just starting or have been doing this for a while, the ideas in the next chapter will be really useful for your journey with Git and GitHub.

CHAPTER 10
Best Practices with Git and GitHub

Introduction

Welcome to *Chapter 10*. In this chapter, you will discover how to communicate well through your commits, the importance of making clear and focused changes in your code storage, and the details of keeping your codebase clean and secure. These practices aren't just about writing better code; they are about creating a more collaborative, organized, and secure development space.

By the end of this chapter, you will have gained invaluable insights and practical skills that will help you use Git and GitHub more effectively and responsibly, ensuring your development practices are not only productive but also secure and in line with industry standards.

Structure

In this chapter, you will learn:

- Crafting Meaningful Commit Messages
- Atomic Commits - One Change Per Commit
- Using `.gitignore` Effectively
- Keeping Sensitive Data Out of Repositories
- Pull Request Etiquettes and Effective Code Reviews

Crafting Meaningful Commit Messages

In software development, good communication is crucial, especially when it comes to commit messages. These short notes, added with each commit, act like a history book that explains why changes were made. The importance of a well-written commit message becomes clear when looking back at changes made months or even years ago. Let's discuss how to make commit messages that make sense and look at the important parts that make them clear and useful.

The Significance of a Commit Message

In the path of software development, emphasizing clear communication has always been important. Nowhere is this more crucial than in the messages that come with each commit. These short notes are not just for show; they act as a historical record that can answer many questions about the reasons behind changes. It's clear how a well-written commit message can make a difference in understanding why changes were made, especially when looking back at modifications from months or years ago.

Anatomy of an Effective Commit Message

Let's talk about structure. The anatomy of a well-structured commit message consists of three parts: **the subject, the body,** and **the footer**.

The Subject Line

This is the headline, the summary of the commit. It should be concise, not more than **50 characters**, and it should succinctly convey the essence of the change.

The Body

The body is where the story unfolds. This is where you explain the "**why**" and "**how**" of the change. The body should be wrapped at **72 characters per line**, which is a conventional width that ensures readability across various tools.

The Footer

This is often used for administrative details, such as referencing issue tracker IDs, co-authoring details, or breaking change notes.

Crafting the Subject Line

The subject line deserves special attention. It's what people see first in the log; it's what stands out in notifications and emails. Using the imperative mood–a command or instruction–is recommended because it's clearer and more direct. It tells what applying the commit will do to the codebase, rather than what you did to the code.

For example, "Fix overflow error in chart rendering" tells the reader that this commit, when applied, fixes an issue. It's active, clear, and direct.

You should keep the following points in mind when creating a subject line:

- Start with a capital letter
- Do not end with a period
- Use the imperative mood
- Be concise yet descriptive

Writing the Body

The body is where the narrative lives. Here's where you explain the problem that existed before and how the commit resolves it. You can also mention why you chose this way, other ideas you thought about, and why you didn't go with them. This is the heart of your commit message – the place where the "**why**" resides.

When writing the body, we often think about the necessary context to understand if we encounter this commit a year from now. Would we understand the reasoning behind the changes? Could we grasp the problem that was being addressed? Would we be able to tell if the change fixed a bug, improved performance, or added a feature? The body of your commit message is your opportunity to answer these questions pre-emptively.

The Footer

While not always necessary, the footer is where you can get into the details that don't belong in the narrative. This could be metadata like "**Closes #34**" or "**See ticket #12 for context.**" It's also where you might acknowledge collaborators who contributed to the commit.

Real-Time Examples

Consider a scenario where you've fixed a bug in a payment processing system that caused transactions to fail due to a timeout issue. Here's how you might document that change:

```git
Ensure timely payment processing on slow networks

Previously, transactions would fail on slow networks because
the timeout was set too aggressively at 5 seconds. This commit
extends the timeout threshold to 15 seconds to accommodate
such conditions, as per the findings from recent user feedback
and error logs analysis. This should reduce transaction failures
and improve user experience during checkout.
```

***Figure 10.1**: Change in document after fixing bug*

In another case, suppose you've added a new feature that allows users to filter search results. Your commit message might look like this:

```
git

Add filter option to search results

Users needed a way to narrow down search results to find items
of interest more quickly. This commit introduces a filter option
based on categories, enabling users to apply multiple filters to
their search query. It extends the search functionality to be more
tailored to user preferences, potentially increasing user engagement.
```

Figure 10.2: *Filter search results*

Why It Matters

Throughout their careers, developers have sometimes overlooked commit messages, treating them as an afterthought. However, when troubleshooting issues or understanding the history of a feature, it's often the quality of commit messages that speeds up comprehension or becomes a roadblock.

Furthermore, in code reviews, clear commit messages make the review process smoother. They give reviewers the context they need to evaluate changes. It's a practice that demonstrates professionalism and consideration for those who will read and work with the code in the future.

By adopting a disciplined approach to writing commit messages, you ensure that your project's history is informative and useful. This practice is a mark of a thoughtful and skilled developer who values the clarity and quality of their work.

Atomic Commits: One Change per Commit

An '**atomic commit**' means that each commit created in a version control system like Git encapsulates a single, self-contained change. This practice is not just about keeping things small for the sake of it; it's about ensuring each piece of work is focused and identifiable.

The Benefits of Atomicity

Why bother breaking down changes into the smallest viable pieces? The benefits are numerous, including:

Easier Code Review

Imagine you're handed a book and asked to find grammatical errors. Now, would you prefer a short story or a dense novel? The same goes for code reviews. Smaller commits make for a more focused and manageable review process. If the changes are small, it's easier for your team to review. They can quickly get what you did and see if anything needs fixing or making it better.

Simpler Troubleshooting

When a bug surfaces, isolating the problem is much easier when each commit is atomic. There was a time when fixing a critical issue only required changing one line. However, because it was hidden among dozens of other changes in a single commit, it took hours to identify. With separate commits, these situations are less time-consuming. You can quickly pinpoint the cause, often with a simple look at the commit log.

Straightforward Reversion

There will be times when a change doesn't work out, and you'll need to revert it. If your commit includes multiple changes, rolling back could mean losing valuable work. However, if you've made your commits atomic, reverting a change is as straightforward as reversing a single commit, leaving the rest of your work intact.

Clear History

The story of your project is told through your commit history. Atomic commits make sure this story is easy to understand. Each commit in the log should be a clear chapter in your project's story, not a confusing mix of plotlines that makes it hard to follow how your code has evolved.

At first, adopting atomic commits might seem like extra effort, especially if you're used to making a bunch of changes at once. But the clarity it brings to your project history is really important. This practice doesn't just help in the present, during code reviews and fixing bugs, but it's also a crucial record for future maintainers of the codebase.

Achieving Atomic Commits

An atomic commit is similar to carefully arranging a toolbox where each tool has a specific purpose. This method of commits makes sure that every change in your collection of code is independent and has a clear, single focus. It's not just about making your history look tidier; it's about making it easier to understand and handle, especially when fixing issues or working together with others.

Here's how you can make your commits atomic:

Stage Thoughtfully

One of the most underrated yet powerful features of Git is the `git add -p` command. This command allows you to stage parts of the changes in your files selectively. For instance, if you've edited a file but only one section of the changes is ready to be committed, `git add -p` lets you add just that section.

Imagine you're editing a script. You've made two changes: one is a bug fix, and the other is a new feature. You can use `git add -p` to add only the bug fix changes to your staging area, leaving the new feature changes for a separate commit.

Commit Frequently

The secret to atomic commits is making small, sensible changes. Instead of waiting for a long list of changes, make it a habit to commit after finishing each small task. This way, your commits stay clear, and the chance of losing your work goes down.

Make it a practice to commit changes every time a function is done or a bug is fixed. This will make it simple to follow progress and find problems when something doesn't work.

Refine Your Changes

Before you save your work, take a look at the changes you made. If something doesn't fit, take it out.

Once, in a project, a team member added a test code along with fixing a problem. This caused confusion when we checked the code. It reminded us how important it is to go through the changes you want to save and make sure each one is clear and focused.

My Experience with Atomic Commits

In the early stages of one of our projects, commits were large and included multiple changes. This caused a significant issue when we discovered a critical bug. We had to spend a lot of time sorting out the commit to find the exact change that caused the issue. Since that day, we started using atomic commits. On numerous occasions, this has saved my team and me countless hours when debugging or understanding the evolution of the codebase.

Atomic commits might seem like a small thing in the development process, but they make a big difference. They encourage good habits, make the code easier to maintain, and create an environment where working together and reviewing code is simpler and more effective. In the next sections, we will look at other practices that, when used with atomic commits, can make the development process really efficient.

Using .gitignore Effectively

The **.gitignore** file in Git is similar to a gatekeeper, determining which files should be kept out of your project repositories. It's not just about keeping things neat; it's making sure only the files you really need are kept track of. This simple tool can make a big difference in how well-organized and clear your repository is.

Setting Up a .gitignore File

In the process of managing a Git repository, it's crucial to filter out unnecessary files from being tracked. Follow this step-by-step guide to set up a .gitignore file, ensuring you exclude files like local configurations, logs, temporary files, or locally installed dependencies.

1. **Identify Unnecessary Files:** Start by identifying files that don't need to be tracked. These could be local configuration files, logs, temporary files, or dependencies that are installed locally. Each project might have different requirements.

2. **Create the .gitignore File:** In the root directory of your Git repository, create a file named **.gitignore**.

3. **Specify the Files and Folders:** Add the names of the files and directories you want to ignore. You can specify patterns using wildcards (*), and ignore all files of a particular type (for example, *.log), or specific files and folders. Comments can be added using **#**.

Example:

```
# Ignore all log files
*.log


# Ignore specific configuration file
config.env


# Ignore a specific directory
node_modules/
```

Strategies for Different Environments

In the changing world of version control, how you deal with ignored files can really affect how clear and efficient your project is. Let's talk about two main ways–Global and Local .gitignore files. We'll also look at why it's important to customize things for your project to have the best version control.

Global versus Local `.gitignore`

- **`Global.gitignore`:** For universally irrelevant files (like operating system files or editor settings), you can set up a global .gitignore that applies to all your projects. This is done by configuring Git to use a global ignore file: `git config --global core.excludesfile '~/.gitignore_global'`.

  The output of the command "`git config --global core.excludesfile '~/.gitignore_global'` " is shown in *Figure* 10.3:

```
PravinMishra@Pravin-MacBook-Pro ~ %git config --global core.excludesfile '~/.gitignore_global'
PravinMishra@Pravin-MacBook-Pro ~ %
```

***Figure* 10.3:** *Output of command "git config --global core. excludesfile '~/.gitignore_global' "*

- **Local .gitignore:** Specific to a project and located in the project's root. It should include files relevant to the project's environment, such as build outputs, language-specific files, and more.

Project-Specific Customization

Each project may require a different set of **ignore rules** depending on the language, frameworks, and tools used. For instance, a Node.js project will typically ignore the **node_modules/** directory, while a Python project might ignore `__pycache__/`.

Effectively using .gitignore is about understanding your project's needs and tailoring the ignore rules to match. It's a practice that, when implemented correctly, saves time and prevents potential issues. It's a small step in setting up a project but goes a long way in maintaining the sanity and efficiency of your repository.

Keeping Sensitive Data Out of Repositories

In software development, it's important to keep important information safe. Things including passwords, API keys, and personal details are crucial for security. When this kind of information gets into version control systems like Git, it becomes a big risk. If sensitive data accidentally gets out, it can cause serious security problems and might even put entire systems in danger.

Best Practices for Protecting Sensitive Data

In the fast-moving world of software development, it's really important to keep important information safe. Let's talk about some best practices to ensure the security and integrity of your repositories.

Awareness and Prevention

The first step is always awareness. Be conscious of what you commit to your repositories. Use **.env** files or environment variables to store sensitive data and reference these in your code. This approach keeps the data out of your codebase and repositories.

Employ .gitignore

A **.gitignore** file is your first line of defence. It should be one of the first files you create in a new repository. Properly configured, it ensures files or directories containing sensitive information are not added to the repository. Common entries in .gitignore files include:

```
# Environment files
.env

# Log files
*.log

# Temporary files
*.tmp
```

Regular Audits

Conduct regular audits of your repositories to check for accidental inclusions of sensitive data. `GitGuardian` and `TruffleHog` are some tools that can scan your repositories for secrets and sensitive data, helping to identify potential vulnerabilities.

Removing Sensitive Data

Even with the best precautions, mistakes can happen. Here's how you can address an accidental commit of sensitive data:

Immediate Response

As soon as you realize sensitive data has been committed, address it immediately. The longer it stays, the higher the risk.

Removing the Data

If the data has been committed but not pushed, you can use git reset to undo the commit. For data that has been pushed, you'll need to use git filter-branch or a tool like the **BFG Repo-Cleaner** to rewrite history and remove the sensitive data. Remember, this alters the history, so you'll need to communicate this with your team to avoid conflicts.

Roll and Invalidate

Once the data is removed from the repository, roll or invalidate the exposed credentials. This means changing passwords or API keys and ensuring the exposed data can no longer grant access to your systems.

Protecting sensitive data in repositories is not just about following a set of rules; it's about cultivating a mindset of security and responsibility. As you progress in your development journey, keep these practices in mind. They are not only protective measures but also essential habits that contribute to the overall integrity and trustworthiness of your software projects.

Pull Request Etiquettes and Effective Code Reviews

Creating a pull request (PR) involves more than simply submitting code for integration; it serves as an invitation for collaboration and feedback. Over the years in software development, the significant impact of well-handled PRs on code quality and team dynamics efficiency has been evident.

Creating a Pull Request

In the collaborative landscape of software development, communication takes center stage, and crafting a meaningful Pull Request (PR) is no exception.

Title and Description

A PR starts with its title and description. These are not mere formalities but the first, a crucial step in effective communication:

- **Title:** This should be concise yet descriptive enough to give a clear idea about the PR's purpose. Think of it as a headline that should capture the essence of your changes.

- **Description:** Here, detail is key. The description should explain the what and the why of your changes. What does this PR accomplish, and why was it necessary? Linking to related issues or tickets is crucial for context.

  Now, we have created Pull request in repository as shown in *Figure 10.4*:

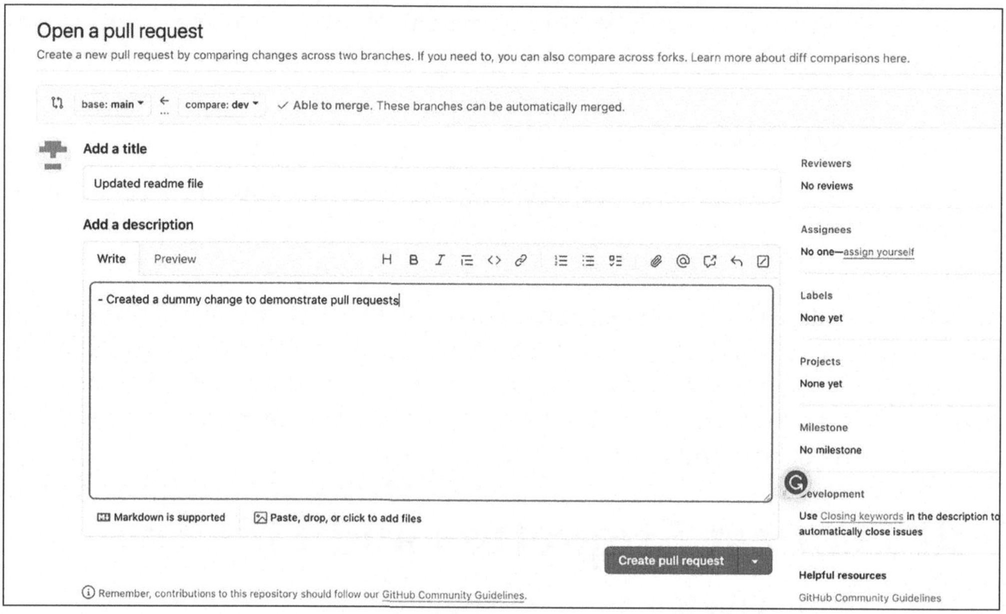

Figure 10.4: *Output of pull request created in GitHub*

Keeping it Small and Focused

One of the most valuable lessons is the power of simplicity in PRs:

- **Size:** Smaller PRs are not just easier to review; they're also easier to manage, test, and integrate. We should always aim for PRs that address a single issue or add a single feature.
- **Focus:** Each PR should have a clear, focused objective. If you find yourself saying "*And it also does...*" it's probably a sign to break it down further.

Self-Review: A Critical Step

Before you click **`'Create Pull Request'`**, take a step back and review your own work.

Go through your changes line by line. Although it might feel boring, it's a chance to find mistakes, make sure everything is the same, and be ready for feedback from those checking your work.

Real-World Example: A Lesson in PR Management

Recalling a project from the early days as a team lead, there was a developer who submitted a huge pull request with lots of new features and bug fixes. The pull request was so big and had so many changes that it was tough to review properly. Problems that could have been easily seen in smaller, focused requests were missed. This caused bugs to sneak into the final product, leading to not just technical issues but also affecting the team's morale.

From this experience, the team learned the importance of breaking down work into smaller, more manageable parts. It wasn't just about making it easier for the people reviewing the work; it was about maintaining good code, simplifying problem tracking, and ensuring smooth integration into the main codebase.

The Ripple Effect of Effective PR Practices

What we learned from that experience was not just a lesson in PR management; it was a lesson in team dynamics and project management. By adopting the practice of creating smaller, more focused PRs, we noticed several improvements such as:

- **Efficient Reviews:** Reviews became quicker and more effective. Reviewers could focus on specific changes without being overwhelmed.
- **Easier Tracking of Issues:** Bugs and issues were easier to trace back to specific changes.
- **Faster Integration:** Smaller changes meant fewer conflicts and easier integration into the main codebase.
- **Team Morale:** Developers felt more confident in their contributions, knowing that their work would receive proper attention and consideration.

In essence, effective pull request creation and code review practices are not just about technical accuracy; they are about fostering a culture of responsibility, attention to detail, and mutual respect. These practices contribute to a healthier codebase and a more collaborative and productive team environment.

Conducting Effective Code Reviews

When reviewing code, it's crucial to remember that your focus should be on the code itself, not the person who wrote it. Any comments made should be about how the work can be improved. This approach not only fosters a positive and productive environment but also ensures that the feedback is taken in the spirit of growth and improvement.

Real-World Application:

Imagine reviewing a piece of code where the error handling is not robust. Instead of commenting, "*You didn't handle potential errors here*," phrase it as "*Adding error handling in this section could improve the reliability of our application.*"

Provide Context

When suggesting changes during a review, it's not enough to just point out what needs to be changed. Explaining why a change is necessary is equally important. This not only helps the author understand your perspective but also turns the review process into a learning experience.

Real-World Application:

If you suggest refactoring a large function into smaller ones, explain that smaller functions are generally easier to read, test, and maintain. This educates the author and others about good coding practices.

Encourage Best Practices

A code review is a perfect opportunity to reinforce adherence to coding standards and best practices. If there's a deviation from these standards, it's important to point it out and provide suggestions for alignment.

Real-World Application:

If a submitted code doesn't follow the established naming conventions or lacks documentation, it needs to be pointed out and referenced to our coding standards. This reinforces the importance of consistency and maintainability in our codebase.

Balancing Speed and Thoroughness

It is important to balance speed and thoroughness by following these practices:

Timely Reviews

In the role of a project leader, understanding the significance of time in the development cycle is crucial. Timely code reviews are essential to prevent bottlenecks. If feedback is delayed, it can result in project delays and be frustrating for the author who is awaiting integration of their changes.

Practical Tip:

Set aside specific times during your day for code reviews to ensure they are done promptly. This helps in managing your workload while also providing timely feedback.

Comprehensive Checks

While it's important to be timely, thoroughness should not be sacrificed. A rushed review can miss critical issues that might affect the project's integrity. Ensure you understand the changes fully and consider their impact on the entire project.

Practical Tip:

Before reviewing, take a moment to understand the context of the changes - what problem does it solve, and how does it fit into the larger picture of the project? This helps in providing a more comprehensive review.

Learning from Each Other

In the collaborative world of software development, learning goes both ways. When you're dealing with code you don't know or wondering about a chosen way of doing things, being curious helps you understand better.

Ask Questions

If something in the code is not clear or you're unsure why a particular approach was chosen, ask. Framing your uncertainty as a question rather than a statement can lead to a constructive dialogue, providing valuable insights into different ways of thinking and problem-solving.

Real-World Application:

In a review, when faced with an unusual method for solving a problem, rather than rejecting it outright, the author is asked to explain their thought process. This prompts a captivating discussion on various approaches, often leading to the discovery of new insights.

Share Knowledge

Code reviews are not just for pointing out what's wrong. They are an excellent opportunity for mutual learning. If you have suggestions or know a better approach, share it. This collaborative approach to reviews not only improves the code but also enhances the team's overall skill set.

Real-World Application:

During a review, when someone notices a chance to make the code simpler by using a design pattern, they explain the pattern and how it can be used in the current situation. This not only makes the code better but also helps the team learn a bit.

Pull requests and code reviews, when done the right way, make the software better and improve the team's skills. They're not just things to be marked as done but important parts of working together on development. By following these etiquettes and practices, teams don't just make better software – they also create a culture of always getting better and continuous learning. In their careers, following these principles has led to faster development, better code, and a team that's more involved and knowledgeable.

Conclusion

In this chapter, we've discussed important ways to use Git and GitHub well. We learned making good commit messages, so it's easy to understand what changes were made. Also, we looked at doing small, focused changes when making commits to keep things organized. These aren't just suggestions – they are important skills for anyone using these tools. We also explored using .gitignore to keep your project tidy, keeping private information out for safety, and having good manners when suggesting changes or reviewing code with pull requests.

These good ways of working are not just also from personal experience but from what the whole development community has learned. They help make your work smoother, encourage teamwork, and keep your code safe. If you make these ways of working a habit, you're building a strong base for quality work in your projects and with your teams.

Index

Symbols

A

B

C

G

I

L

M

O

P

R

S

T

V